Unity Artificial Intelligence Programming
Fourth Edition

Add powerful, believable, and fun AI entities in your game
with the power of Unity 2018!

Dr. Davide Aversa
Aung Sithu Kyaw
Clifford Peters

BIRMINGHAM - MUMBAI

Unity Artificial Intelligence Programming
Fourth Edition

Commissioning Editor: Amarabha Banerjee
Acquisition Editor: Larissa Pinto
Content Development Editor: Keagan Carneiro
Technical Editor: Ralph Rosario
Copy Editor: Safis Editing
Project Coordinator: Pragati Shukla
Proofreader: Safis Editing
Indexer: Rekha Nair
Graphics: Alishon Mendonsa
Production Coordinator: Shantanu Zagade

First published: July 2013
Second edition: September 2015
Third edition: January 2018
Fourth edition: November 2018

Production reference: 1301118

Published by Packt Publishing Ltd.
Livery Place
35 Livery Street
Birmingham
B3 2PB, UK.

ISBN 978-1-78953-391-0

www.packtpub.com

To Gioia, my special one, because through the calm or rough sea, you are and always will be my lighthouse.

- Davide Aversa

`mapt.io`

Mapt is an online digital library that gives you full access to over 5,000 books and videos, as well as industry leading tools to help you plan your personal development and advance your career. For more information, please visit our website.

Why subscribe?

- Spend less time learning and more time coding with practical eBooks and Videos from over 4,000 industry professionals

- Improve your learning with Skill Plans built especially for you

- Get a free eBook or video every month

- Mapt is fully searchable

- Copy and paste, print, and bookmark content

Packt.com

Did you know that Packt offers eBook versions of every book published, with PDF and ePub files available? You can upgrade to the eBook version at `www.packt.com` and as a print book customer, you are entitled to a discount on the eBook copy. Get in touch with us at `customercare@packtpub.com` for more details.

At `www.packt.com`, you can also read a collection of free technical articles, sign up for a range of free newsletters, and receive exclusive discounts and offers on Packt books and eBooks.

Contributors

About the authors

Dr. Davide Aversa holds a Ph.D. in Artificial Intelligence and an M.Sc. in Artificial Intelligence and Robotics from the University of Rome "La Sapienza" in Italy. He has a strong interest in Artificial Intelligence for the development of Interactive Virtual Agents and Procedural Content Generation (PCG). He serves at the PC of videogame-related conferences such as the IEEE Conference on Computational Intelligence and Games (CIG) and he also is regularly participating in game-jam contests. He also writes a blog on Game Design and game development.

I would like to thank my family for supporting me during the work on this book. I want to thank my employer for giving me the time to write this book. Finally, I would also like to thanks the editors at Packt for driving me through this challenging experience and for being understanding of my delays.

Aung Sithu Kyaw is passionate about graphics programming, creating video games, writing, and sharing knowledge with others. He holds an MSc degree in digital media technology from the Nanyang Technological University (NTU), Singapore. He worked as a research associate, which involved implementing a sensor-based real-time movie system using Unreal Development Kit. In 2011, he founded a tech start-up focusing on interactive media productions and backend server-side technologies.

Clifford Peters is a programmer and a computer scientist. He has reviewed the following Packt Publishing books: *Unity Game Development Essentials, Unity 3D Game Development by Example Beginner's Guide, Unity 3 Game Development Hotshot, Unity 3.x Game Development by Example Beginner's Guide, Unity iOS Game Development Beginner's Guide,* and *Unity iOS Essentials.*

About the reviewer

Deepak Jadhav is a Game Developer based in Pune, India. Deepak received his Bachelor's Degree in Computer Technology and Master's Degree in Game Programming and Project Management. Currently, He is working as Game Developer in the leading game development company in India. He has been involved in developing games on multiple platforms, such as PC, Mac, mobile. With years of experience in game development, he has a strong background in C# and C++, as well as he has built up skills in platforms including Unity, Unreal Engine, Augmented and Virtual Reality.

> *I would like to thank my family and friends for the continued support at every turn in my life. I also like to thank Author and Packt Publishing for giving me the opportunity to review this book.*

Packt is searching for authors like you

If you're interested in becoming an author for Packt, please visit `authors.packtpub.com` and apply today. We have worked with thousands of developers and tech professionals, just like you, to help them share their insight with the global tech community. You can make a general application, apply for a specific hot topic that we are recruiting an author for, or submit your own idea.

Table of Contents

Preface

This book is meant to help you to incorporate various **Artificial Intelligence (AI)** techniques into your games. We will discuss decision techniques such as **Finite State Machines (FSMs)** and behavior trees. We will also look at movement, obstacle avoidance, and flocking. We also show how to follow a path, how to create a path using the A* pathfinding algorithm, and then how to reach a destination using a navigation mesh. As a bonus, we will go into detail about randomness and probability, and then incorporate these ideas into a final project.

Who this book is for

This book is for anyone who wants to learn about incorporating AI into games. This book is intended for users with prior experience of using Unity. We will be coding in C#, so some familiarity with this language is expected.

What this book covers

Chapter 1, *Introduction to AI*, talks about what AI is and how it is used in games. Also, we talk about the various techniques used to implement AI into games.

Chapter 2, *Finite State Machines*, discusses a way of simplifying how we manage the decisions that AI needs to make. We use FSMs to determine how AI behaves in a particular state and how it transitions to other states.

Chapter 3, *Randomness and Probability*, discusses the basics behind probability and how to change the probability of a particular outcome. Then we look at how to add randomness to our game to make the AI less predictable.

Chapter 4, *Implementing Sensors*, looks at making our character aware of the world around them. With the ability of our characters to see and hear, they will know when an enemy is nearby and will know when to attack or defend themselves.

Chapter 5, *Flocking*, discusses a situation where many objects travel together as a group. We will look at two different ways to implement flocking and how it can be used to make objects move together.

Chapter 6, *Path Following and Steering Behaviors*, looks at how AI characters can follow a path provided to reach a destination. Then we look at how AI characters can find a target without knowing a path and move toward a goal while avoiding danger.

Chapter 7, *A* Pathfinding*, discusses a popular algorithm that is used to find the best route from a given location to a target location. With A*, we scan the terrain and find the best path that leads us to the goal.

Chapter 8, *Navigation Mesh*, discusses using the power of Unity to make pathfinding easier to implement. By creating a navigation mesh, we will be able to represent the scene around us better than we could using tiles and the A* algorithm.

Chapter 9, *Behavior Trees*, expands FSMs into something we can use for even the most complex of games. We will be using the free plugin called Behavior Bricks to help us create and manage behavior trees in Unity.

Chapter 10, *Machine Learning*, explores how to apply machine learning (in particular, reinforcement learning) to game characters for games or simulations. We will use the official Unity's ML-Agent Toolkit. In the first part, we will learn how to configure Unity and the external requirements for the toolkit. Then we will showcase a simple practical example.

Chapter 11, *Putting It All Together*, takes various elements of what we have learned throughout the book to put together one last project. Here you will be able to apply the remaining AI elements that we will have learned about and create an impressive vehicular battle game.

To get the most out of this book

The main requirement for this book is having Unity Version 2018.2 or higher installed. In Chapter 9, *Behavior Trees*, we download Behavior Bricks, a free Behavior Tree plugin, which requires an account with the Unity Store. In Chapter 10, *Machine Learning*, we will use Unity's Machine Learning for Agents Toolkit, an official machine learning platform based on TensorFlow. For this reason, that chapter requires Python 3.6 to be installed.

Download the example code files

You can download the example code files for this book from your account at www.packt.com. If you purchased this book elsewhere, you can visit www.packt.com/support and register to have the files emailed directly to you.

You can download the code files by following these steps:

1. Log in or register at www.packt.com.
2. Select the **SUPPORT** tab.
3. Click on **Code Downloads & Errata**.
4. Enter the name of the book in the **Search** box and follow the onscreen instructions.

Once the file is downloaded, please make sure that you unzip or extract the folder using the latest version of:

- WinRAR/7-Zip for Windows
- Zipeg/iZip/UnRarX for Mac
- 7-Zip/PeaZip for Linux

The code bundle for the book is also hosted on GitHub at https://github.com/PacktPublishing/Unity-Artificial-Intelligence-Programming-Fourth-Edition. In case there's an update to the code, it will be updated on the existing GitHub repository.

We also have other code bundles from our rich catalog of books and videos available at https://github.com/PacktPublishing/. Check them out!

Download the color images

We also provide a PDF file that has color images of the screenshots/diagrams used in this book. You can download it here: https://www.packtpub.com/sites/default/files/downloads/9781789533910_ColorImages.pdf.

Conventions used

In this book, you will find a number of styles of text that distinguish between different kinds of information. Here are some examples of these styles, and an explanation of their meaning.

Code words in text are shown as follows: "The AdvanceFSM class basically manages all the FSMState(s) implemented, and keeps updated with the transitions and the current state."

A block of code is set as follows:

```
int throwDiceLoaded() {
    Debug.Log("Throwing dice...");
        int randomProbability = Random.Range(1,101);
        int diceResult = 0;
        if (randomProbability < 36) {
          diceResult = 6;
        }
        else {
          diceResult = Random.Range(1,5);
        }
    Debug.Log("Result: " + diceResult);
        return diceResult;
    }
```

New terms and important words are shown in bold. Words that you see on the screen, in menus or dialog boxes for example, appear in the text like this: "Our Tank object is basically a simple **Mesh** with a **Rigidbody** component."

 Warnings or important notes appear like this.

 Tips and tricks appear like this.

Get in touch

Feedback from our readers is always welcome.

General feedback: If you have questions about any aspect of this book, mention the book title in the subject of your message and email us at customercare@packtpub.com.

Errata: Although we have taken every care to ensure the accuracy of our content, mistakes do happen. If you have found a mistake in this book, we would be grateful if you would report this to us. Please visit www.packt.com/submit-errata, selecting your book, clicking on the Errata Submission Form link, and entering the details.

Piracy: If you come across any illegal copies of our works in any form on the Internet, we would be grateful if you would provide us with the location address or website name. Please contact us at copyright@packt.com with a link to the material.

If you are interested in becoming an author: If there is a topic that you have expertise in and you are interested in either writing or contributing to a book, please visit authors.packtpub.com.

Reviews

Please leave a review. Once you have read and used this book, why not leave a review on the site that you purchased it from? Potential readers can then see and use your unbiased opinion to make purchase decisions, we at Packt can understand what you think about our products, and our authors can see your feedback on their book. Thank you!

For more information about Packt, please visit packt.com.

Introduction to AI 1

This chapter will give you a little background on **Artificial Intelligence (AI)** in academic, traditional domains, and game specific applications. We'll learn how the application and implementation of AI in games is different from other domains, and the essential and unique requirements for AI in games. We'll also explore the basic techniques of AI used in games. This chapter will serve as a reference for later chapters, where we'll implement these AI techniques in Unity.

In this chapter, we'll cover the following topics:

- Artificial Intelligence (AI)
- AI in games
- AI techniques

Artificial Intelligence (AI)

Living organisms, such as animals and humans, naturally have some level of intelligence that allows them to be able to take meaningful decisions during their daily lives. On the other hand, computers are just electronic devices that can accept data, perform logical and mathematical operations at high speeds, and output the results. AI is essentially the subject of making computers able to think and decide like living organisms to perform specific operations.

As you can imagine, this is a huge subject. There's no way that such a small book will be able to cover everything related to AI. However, it is essential to understand how to use the basics of AI in different domains. AI is just a general term; its implementations and applications are different for different purposes, solving different sets of problems.

Before we move on to game-specific techniques, we'll take a look at some of the research areas in AI applications:

- **Computer vision**: This is the ability to take visual input from sources such as videos and cameras, and analyze them to do particular operations such as facial recognition, object recognition, and optical character recognition.
- **Natural Language Processing (NLP)**: This is the ability that allows a machine to read and understand human languages, that is, as we usually write and speak. The problem is that human languages are difficult for machines to understand. Language ambiguity is the main problem: there are many different ways to say the same thing, and the same sentence can have different meanings according to the context. NLP is a significant step for machines since they need to understand the languages and expressions we use before they can process them and respond accordingly. Fortunately, there's an enormous amount of datasets available on the web that can help researchers to automate the analysis of a language.
- **Common sense reasoning**: This is a technique that our brains can efficiently use to draw answers, even from the domains we don't fully understand. Common sense knowledge is a standard way for us to attempt several questions since our brains can mix and interplay between the context, background knowledge, and language proficiency. Unfortunately, making machines to apply such knowledge is very complicated, and still a significant challenge for researchers.

AI in games

Game AI needs to complement the quality of a game. For that, we need to understand the fundamental requirement that every game must have. The answer should be easy: the fun factor. So, what makes a game fun to play? Answering this question is the subject of game design, and a good reference is *The Art of Game Design* by Jesse Schell. Let's attempt to tackle this question without going deep into game design topics. We'll find that a challenging game is indeed fun to play. Let me repeat: it's about making a game challenging. This means the game should not be so difficult that it's impossible for the player to beat the opponent, or too easy to win. Finding the right challenge level is the key to making a game fun to play.

And that's where the AI kicks in. The role of AI in games is to make it fun by providing challenging opponents to compete, and interesting **Non-Player Characters** (**NPCs**) that behave realistically inside the game world. So, the objective here is not to replicate the whole thought process of humans or animals, but to make the NPCs seem intelligent by reacting to the changing situations inside the game world, in a way that makes sense to the player.

The reason that we don't want to make the AI system in games so computationally expensive is that the processing power required for AI calculations needs to be shared between other operations, such as graphics rendering and physics simulation. Also, don't forget that they are all happening in real time, and it's critical to achieving a steady frame rate throughout the game. There were even attempts to create a dedicated processor for AI calculations (AI seek's Intia Processor or the Google's Tensorflow processing unit). With the ever-increasing processing power, we now have more and more room for AI calculations. However, like all of the other disciplines in game development, optimizing AI calculations remains a considerable challenge for the AI developers.

AI techniques

In this section, we'll walk through some of the AI techniques commonly used in different types of games. We'll learn how to implement each of these features in Unity in the upcoming chapters. Since this book is not focused on AI techniques themselves, but the implementation of these techniques inside Unity, we won't go into too much detail about these techniques here. So, let's just take it as a crash course, before actually going into implementation. If you want to learn more about AI for games, there are some really great books out there, such as *Programming Game AI by Example* by Mat Buckland and *Artificial Intelligence for Games* by Ian Millington and John Funge. The *AI Game Programming Wisdom* and *Game AI Pro* series also contain a lot of useful resources and articles on the latest AI techniques.

Finite State Machines (FSMs)

Finite State Machines (**FSMs**) are one of the simplest AI model forms and are commonly used in the majority of games. A state machine consists of a finite number of states that are connected in a graph by the transitions between them. A game entity starts with an initial state and then looks out for the events and rules that will trigger a transition to another state. A game entity can only be in exactly one state at any given time.

For example, let's take a look at an AI guard character in a typical shooting game. Its states could be as simple as patrolling, chasing, and shooting:

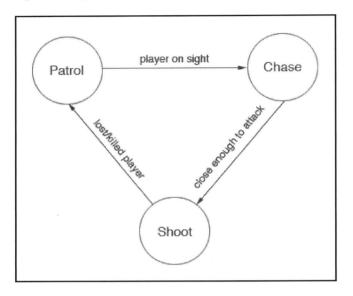

Simple FSM of an AI guard character

There are four components in a simple FSM:

- **States**: This component defines a set of states that a game entity or an NPC can choose from (**Patrol**, **Chase**, and **Shoot**)
- **Transitions**: This component defines relations between different states
- **Rules**: This component is used to trigger a state transition (**player on sight**, **close enough to attack**, and **lost/killed player**)
- **Events**: This is the component that will trigger to check the rules (guard's visible area, distance with the player, and so on)

So, a monster in *Quake 2* might have the following states: standing, walking, running, dodging, attacking, idle, and searching.

FSMs are widely used in game AI because they are simple to implement and more than enough for both simple and somewhat complex games. Using simple `if/else` statements or switch statements, we can quickly implement an FSM. On the other hand, they can get messy when we start to have a lot of states and transitions. We'll look at how to manage a simple FSM in the next chapter.

Random and probability in AI

Imagine an enemy bot in a **First Person Shooter** (**FPS**) game that can always kill the player with a headshot, an opponent in a racing game that always chooses the best route and overtakes without collision with any obstacle. Such a level of intelligence will make the game so hard that it becomes almost impossible to win and thus frustrating. On the opposite side of the spectrum, imagine an AI enemy that always chooses the same route when it tries to escape from or attack the player. AI controlled entities behaving the same way every time the player encounters them, make the game predictable, easy to win, and therefore boring.

Both of the previous situations affect the fun aspect of the game and make the player feel like the game is not challenging or fair enough anymore. One way to fix this sort of perfect AI and stupid AI is to introduce some intentional mistakes in their behavior. In games, randomness and probabilities are applied in the decision-making process of AI calculations. The following are the main situations when we would want to let our AI take a random decision:

- **Non-intentional**: In some situations, an NPC might need to make a decision randomly, just because it doesn't have enough information to make a perfect decision, and/or it doesn't really matter what decision it makes. Just making a decision randomly and hoping for the best result is a perfect solution in many real-world situations.
- **Intentional**: As we discussed in the previous examples, we will need to add some randomness purposely to make them more realistic, and also to match a difficulty level that suits the player. We can use randomness for things such as hit probabilities, add or subtract a certain random damage on top of base damage, or make an NPC hesitate before start shooting. Using randomness and probability, we can add a sense of realistic uncertainty to our game and make our AI system more fair and/or unpredictable.

The sensor system

Our AI characters need to know about their surroundings and the world they are interacting with in order to make a particular decision. Such information may be the following:

- **The position of the player**: This is used to decide whether to attack or chase, or keep patrolling
- **Buildings and objects nearby**: This is used to hide or take cover

- **Player's health and its own health**: This is used to decide whether to retreat or advance
- **Location of resources on the map in a Real-Time Strategy game (RTS)**: This is used to occupy and collect resources required for updating and/or producing other units

As you can see, choosing the right method to collect game information can vary a lot depending on the type of game we are trying to build. In the following sections, we look at two basic strategies: **polling** and **message (event) systems**.

Polling

One method to collect such information is polling. Polling consists of directly checking for the preceding information in the `FixedUpdate` method of our AI character. An AI character can just poll the information they are interested in from the game world, do the checks, and take action accordingly. Polling works great if there aren't too many things to check. To make this method more efficient, we may program some characters to poll the world states with different polling rates so that we do not stop polling at every frame for every character. However, as soon as the game gets bigger, polling is not enough anymore. Therefore, in more massive games with more complex AI systems, we need to deploy an event-driven method using a global messaging system.

The messaging system

AI does decision making in response to the events in the world. The events are communicated between the AI entity and the player, the world, or the other AI entities through a messaging system. For example, when the player attacks an enemy unit from a group of patrol guards, the other AI units need to know about this incident as well, so that they can start searching for and attacking the player. If we were using the polling method, our AI entities would need to check the state of all of the other AI entities to know about this incident. However, with an event-driven messaging system, we can implement this in a more manageable and scalable way. We can register the AI characters interested in a particular event as listeners, and if that event happens, our messaging system will broadcast to all listeners. The AI entities can then proceed to take appropriate actions or perform further checks.

The event-driven system does not necessarily provide a faster mechanism than polling. Still, it provides a convenient, central checking system that senses the world and informs the interested AI agents, rather than each agent having to check the same event in every frame. In reality, both polling and messaging systems are used together most of the time. For example, AI might poll for more detailed information when it receives an event from the messaging system.

Flocking, swarming, and herding

Many living beings such as birds, fish, insects, and land animals perform specific operations such as moving, hunting, and foraging in groups. They stay and hunt in groups because it makes them stronger and safer from predators than pursuing goals individually. So, let's say you want a group of birds flocking, swarming around in the sky; it'll cost too much time and effort for animators to design the movement and animations of each bird. However, if we apply some simple rules for each bird to follow, we can achieve the emergent intelligence of the whole group with complex, global behavior.

One pioneer of this concept is Craig Reynolds, who presented such a flocking algorithm in his 1987 SIGGRAPH paper, *Flocks, Herds, and Schools – A Distributed Behavioral Model*. He coined the term *boid* that sounds like *bird*, but refer to a *bird-like* object. He proposed three simple rules to apply to each unit:

- **Separation**: Each boid needs to maintain a minimum distance with neighboring boids to avoid hitting them (short-range repulsion)
- **Alignment**: Each boid needs to align itself with the average direction of its neighbors, and then move in the same velocity with them as a flock
- **Cohesion**: Each boid is attracted to the group's center of mass (long-range attraction)

These three simple rules are all that we need to implement a realistic and a reasonably complex flocking behavior for birds. We can also apply them to group behaviors of any other entity type with little or no modifications. We'll examine how to implement such a flocking system in Unity in `Chapter 5`, *Flocking*.

Path following and steering

Sometimes we want our AI characters to roam around in the game world, following a roughly guided or thoroughly defined path. For example, in a racing game, the AI opponents need to navigate on the road, and the simple reactive algorithms, such as our flocking boid algorithm discussed already, are not powerful enough to solve this problem. Still, in the end, it all comes down to dealing with actual movements and steering behaviors. Steering behaviors for AI characters have been in research topics for a couple of decades now. One notable paper in this field is *Steering Behaviors for Autonomous Characters*, again by Craig Reynolds, presented in 1999 at the **Game Developers Conference** (**GDC**). He categorized steering behaviors into the following three layers:

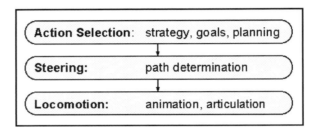

Hierarchy of motion behaviors

Let me quote the original example from his paper to understand these three layers:

Consider, for example, some cowboys tending a herd of cattle out on the range. A cow wanders away from the herd. The trail boss tells a cowboy to fetch the stray. The cowboy says *giddy-up* to his horse, and guides it to the cow, possibly avoiding obstacles along the way. In this example, the trail boss represents action selection, noticing that the state of the world has changed (a cow left the herd), and setting a goal (retrieve the stray). The steering level is represented by the cowboy who decomposes the goal into a series of simple sub goals (approach the cow, avoid obstacles, and retrieve the cow). A sub-goal corresponds to a steering behavior for the cowboy-and-horse team. Using various control signals (vocal commands, spurs, and reins), the cowboy steers his horse towards the target. In general terms, these signals express concepts such as go faster, go slower, turn right, turn left, and so on. The horse implements the locomotion level. Taking the cowboy's control signals as input, the horse moves in the indicated direction. This motion is the result of a complex interaction of the horse's visual perception, its sense of balance, and its muscles applying torque to the joints of its skeleton.

Then he presented how to design and implement some common and straightforward steering behaviors for individual AI characters and pairs. Such behaviors include *seek* and *flee, pursue,* and *evade, wander, arrival, obstacle avoidance, wall following,* and *path following.* We'll implement some of those behaviors in Unity in Chapter 6, *Path Following and Steering Behaviors.*

A* pathfinding

There are many games where you can find monsters or enemies that follow the player or go to a particular point while avoiding obstacles. For example, let's take a look at a typical RTS game. You can select a group of units and click a location where you want them to move or click on the enemy units to attack them. Your units then need to find a way to reach the goal without colliding with the obstacles. The enemy units also need to be able to do the same. Obstacles could be different for different units. For example, an air force unit might be able to pass over a mountain, while the ground or artillery units need to find a way around it.

A * (pronounced *A star*) is a pathfinding algorithm widely used in games because of its performance, accuracy, and ease of implementation. Let's take a look at an example to see how it works. Let's say we want our unit to move from point **A** to point **B**, but there's a wall in the way, and it can't go straight towards the target. So, it needs to find a way to point **B** while avoiding the wall:

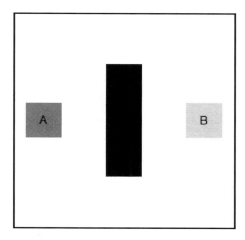

Top-down view of our map

We are looking at a simple 2D example, but we can apply the same idea to 3D environments. In order to find the path from point **A** to point **B**, we need to know more about the map, such as the position of obstacles. For that, we can split our whole map into small tiles representing the whole map in a grid format, as shown in the following diagram:

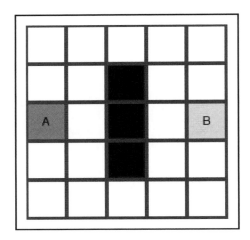

Map represented in a 2D grid

The tiles can also be of other shapes such as hexagons and triangles, but we'll use square tiles here because they are the most natural solution. By representing the whole map as a grid, we simplify the search area: an important step in pathfinding.

We can now reference our map in a small 2D array.

We represent our map with a 5 x 5 grid of square tiles for a total of 25 tiles. Now, we can start searching for the best path to reach the target. How do we do this? By calculating the movement score of each tile adjacent to the starting tile that is not occupied by an obstacle, and then choosing the tile with the lowest cost.

If we don't consider the diagonal movements, there are four possible adjacent tiles to the player. Now, we need to know two numbers to calculate the movement score for each of those tiles. Let's call them G and H, where G is the cost to move from starting tile to current tile, and H is the *estimated* cost to reach the target tile from the current tile.

Let's call F the sum of *G* and *H*, ($F = G + H$); that is the final score of that tile:

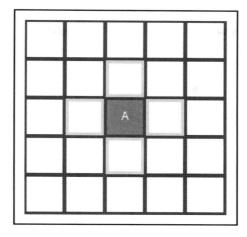

Valid adjacent tiles

In our example, to estimate *H*, we'll be using a simple method called **Manhattan length** (also known as **taxicab geometry**). According to this method, the distance (cost) between tiles **A** and **B** is just the minimum number of tiles between **A** and **B**:

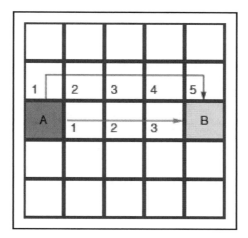

Calculating G

The G value, instead, represents the *cost so far* during the search. The preceding diagram shows the calculations of G with two different paths. To compute the current G, we just add one (which is the cost to move one tile) to the previous tile's G score. However, we can give different costs to different tiles. For example, we might want to give a higher movement cost for diagonal movements (if we are considering them), or to specific tiles occupied by, let's say a pond or a muddy road.

Now we know how to get G. Let's look at the calculation of H. The following diagram shows different H values from different starting tiles to the target tile. As we said before, we are just computing the Manhattan length between the current tile and the goal:

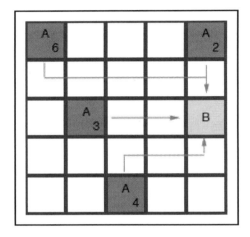

Calculating H

So, now we know how to get G and H. Let's go back to our original example to figure out the shortest path from **A** to **B**. We first choose the starting tile, and then determine the valid adjacent tiles, as shown in the following diagram. Then we calculate the G and H scores of each tile, shown in the lower left and right corners of the tile respectively. Therefore the final score F, which is $G + H$ is shown at the top-left corner. Obviously, the tile to the immediate right of the start tile has got the lowest F score.

So, we choose this tile as our next movement and store the previous tile as its parent. Keeping records of parents will be useful later when we trace back our final path:

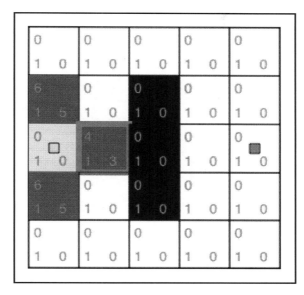

Starting position

From the current tile, we do the similar process again, determining valid adjacent tiles. This time there are only two valid adjacent tiles at the top and bottom. The left tile is the starting tile—which we've already examined—and the obstacle occupies the right tile. We calculate the G, the H, and then the F score of those new adjacent tiles. This time we have four tiles on our map with all having the same score: six. So, which one do we choose? We can choose any of them. It doesn't really matter in this example, because we'll eventually find the shortest path with whichever tile we choose as long they have the same score. Usually, we simply choose the tile added most recently to our adjacent list. Later we'll be using a data structure, such as a list, to store the *next move* candidate tiles. So, accessing the tile most recently added to that list could be faster than searching through the list to reach a particular tile that was added previously.

In this demo, we'll randomly choose the tile for our next test, to prove that it can still find the shortest path:

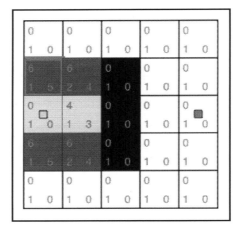

Second step

So, we choose the tile highlighted with a red border. Again, we examine the adjacent tiles. In this step, there's only one new adjacent tile with a calculated F score of 8. So, the lowest score right now is still 6. We can choose any tile with the score 6:

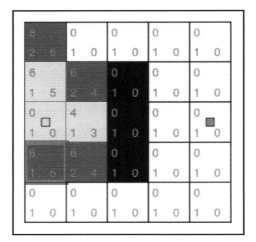

Third step

So, we choose a tile randomly from all the tiles with the score 6. If we repeat this process until we reach our target tile, we'll end up with a board complete with all the scores for each valid tile:

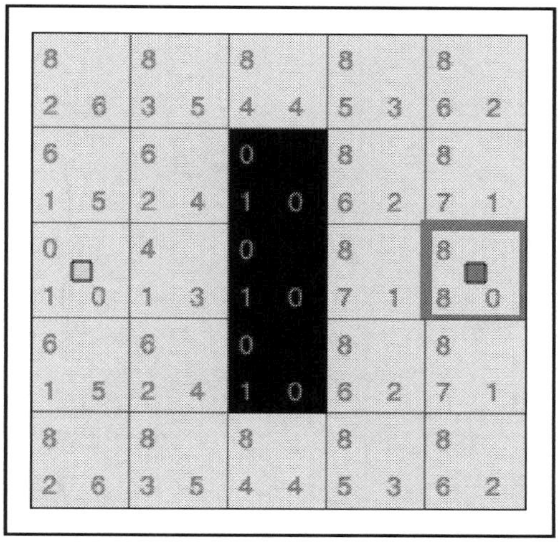

8	8	8	8	8
2 6	3 5	4 4	5 3	6 2
6	6	0	8	8
1 5	2 4	1 0	6 2	7 1
0	4	0	8	8
1 0	1 3	1 0	7 1	8 0
6	6	0	8	8
1 5	2 4	1 0	6 2	7 1
8	8	8	8	8
2 6	3 5	4 4	5 3	6 2

Reach target

Now, all we have to do is to trace back starting from the target tile using its parent tile. In the end, we obtain a path that looks something like the following diagram:

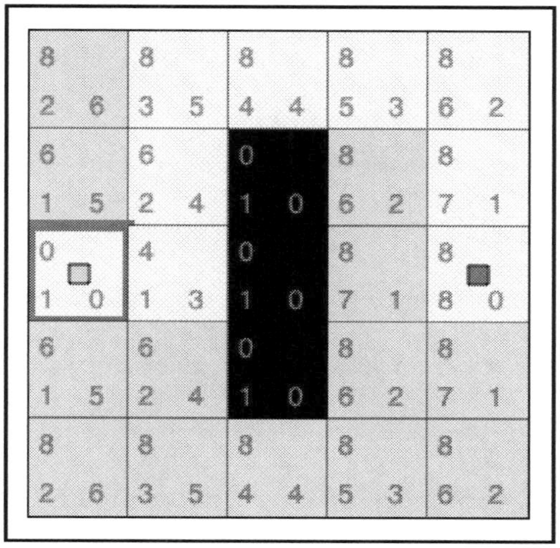

8	8	8	8	8
2 6	3 5	4 4	5 3	6 2
6	6	0	8	8
1 5	2 4	1 0	6 2	7 1
0	4	0	8	8
1 0	1 3	1 0	7 1	8 0
6	6	0	8	8
1 5	2 4	1 0	6 2	7 1
8	8	8	8	8
2 6	3 5	4 4	5 3	6 2

Path traced back

What we explained here is the essence of A* pathfinding without displaying any code. A* is a central concept in pathfinding. Fortunately, since Unity 3.5, there are a couple of new features such as automatic navigation mesh generation and the Nav Mesh Agent, which make implementing pathfinding in your games very much more accessible. In fact, you may not even need to know about A* to implement pathfinding for your AI characters. Nonetheless, knowing how the system is working behind the scenes is essential to becoming a solid AI programmer.

We'll talk about Nav Mesh roughly in the next section and then in more detail in Chapter 8, *Navigation Mesh.*

A navigation mesh

Now we have some idea of A* pathfinding techniques. One thing that you might notice is that using a simple grid in A* requires quite a few computations steps to get a path which is the shortest to the target and at the same time avoids the obstacles. It may not seem notable, but for huge maps with thousands of tiles, searching for a path tile-by-tile in a mostly empty map is a severe waste of computational power. So, to make it cheaper and faster for AI characters to find a path, people came up with the idea of using waypoints as a guide to move AI characters from the start point to the target point. Let's say we want to move our AI character from point **A** to point **B**, and we've set up three waypoints, as shown in the following diagram:

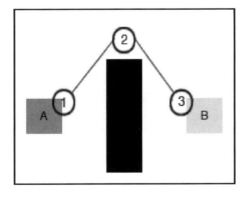

Waypoints

All we have to do now is to pick up the nearest waypoint, and then follow its connected node leading to the target waypoint. Most of the games use waypoints for pathfinding because they are simple and quite effective in using fewer computation resources. However, they do have some issues. What if we want to update the obstacles in our map? We'll also have to place waypoints for the updated map again, as shown in the following diagram:

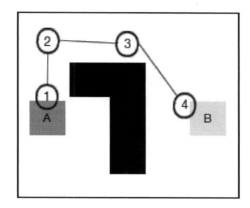

New waypoints

Following each node to the target can mean the AI character moves in zigzag directions. Look at the preceding diagrams; it's quite likely that the AI character will collide with the wall where the path is close to the wall. If that happens, our AI will keep trying to go through the wall to reach the next target, but it won't be able to, and it will get stuck there. Even though we can smooth out the zigzag path by transforming it to a spline and make some adjustments to avoid such obstacles, the problem is the waypoints don't give any information about the environment, other than the spline connects between two nodes. What if our smoothed and adjusted path passes the edge of a cliff or a bridge? The new path might not be a safe path anymore. So, for our AI entities to be able to traverse the whole level effectively, we're going to need a tremendous number of waypoints, which is very hard to implement and manage.

Let's look at a better solution, navigation mesh. A navigation mesh is another graph structure that can be used to represent our world, similar to the way we did with our square tile-based grid or waypoints graph:

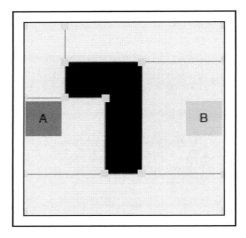

Navigation mesh

A navigation mesh uses convex polygons to represent the areas in the map that an AI entity can travel. The most important benefit of using a navigation mesh is that it gives a lot more information about the environment than a waypoint system. Now we can adjust our path safely because we know the safe region in which our AI entities can travel. Another advantage of using a navigation mesh is that we can use the same mesh for different types of AI entities. Different AI entities can have different properties such as size, speed, and movement abilities. For instance, a set of waypoints may be tailored for human, and they may not work nicely for flying creatures or AI controlled vehicles. Those might need different sets of waypoints. Using a navigation mesh can save a lot of time in such cases.

However, programmatically generating a navigation mesh based on a scene is a somewhat complicated process. Fortunately, Unity includes a built-in navigation mesh generator. Since this is not a book on core AI techniques, we won't go too much into how to generate and use such navigation meshes. Instead, we'll learn how to use Unity's navigation mesh for generating features to implement our AI pathfinding efficiently.

The behavior trees

Behavior trees are the other techniques used to represent and control the logic behind AI characters. They have become popular for the applications in AAA games such as *Halo* and *Spore*. Previously, we have briefly covered FSMs. FSMs provide a straightforward way to define the logic of an AI character, based on the different states and transitions between them. However, FSMs are considered challenging to scale and reuse. To support all the scenarios which we want our AI character to consider, we need to add many states and hardwire many transitions. So, we need a more scalable approach when dealing with more extensive problems. Behavior trees are a better way to implement AI game characters that could potentially become more and more complex.

The basic elements of behavior trees are tasks, where states are the main elements for FSMs. Tasks are linked together by control flow nodes in a tree-like structure. There are many commonly used nodes such as **Sequence**, **Selector**, and **Parallel Decorator** while tasks are the leaves of the tree. For example, let's try to translate our example from the FSM section using a behavior tree. We can break all the transitions and states into basic tasks:

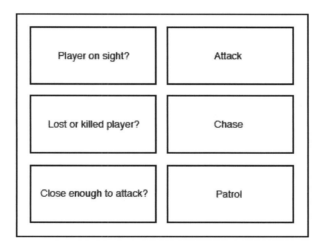

Tasks

Let's look at a Selector node for this behavior tree. Selector nodes usually are represented with a circle and a question mark inside. A Selector node tries to execute all the child tasks/sub-trees in order until one of them succeeds. First, it'll choose to attack the player. If the **Attack** task returns success, the Selector node is completed, and it goes back to the parent node—if there is one. If the **Attack** task fails, it'll try the **Chase** task. Finally, if the **Chase** task fails, it'll try the **Patrol** task:

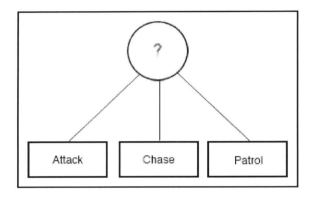

Selector task

What about the tests? They are also one of the tasks in the behavior trees. The following diagram shows the use of Sequence nodes, denoted by a rectangle with an arrow inside it. The root Selector starts with the first Sequence action. This Sequence action's first task is to check whether the player character is close enough to attack. If this task succeeds, it'll proceed with the next task, which is to attack the player. If the **Attack** task also returns success, the whole Sequence returns success, and the Selector is done with this behavior, and it does not continue with other Sequence nodes. If the **Close enough to attack?** task fails, then the Sequence action does not proceed to the **Attack** task and returns a failed status to the parent Selector node. Then the Selector chooses the next task in the Sequence, **Lost or Killed Player**:

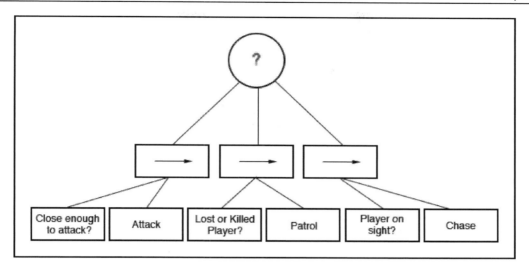

Sequence tasks

The other two common nodes are Parallel and Decorator. A Parallel node executes all of its child tasks at the same time, while the Sequence and Selector nodes only execute their child tasks one by one. A Decorator is another type of node that has only one child. It can change the behavior of its own child's tasks, which includes whether to run its child's task or not, how many times it should run, and so on.

We'll look into more details and study how to implement a basic behavior tree system in Unity in Chapter 9, *Behavior Trees*.

Locomotion

Animals (including humans) have a very complex musculoskeletal system (the locomotor system) that gives them the ability to move around the body using the muscular and skeletal systems. We know where to put our steps when climbing a ladder, stairs, or on uneven terrain, and we know how to balance our body to stabilize all the fancy poses we want to make. We can do all this using our bones, muscles, joints, and other tissues, collectively described as our locomotor system.

Now, put that into our game development perspective. Let's say we have a human character who needs to walk on both even and uneven surfaces, or on small slopes, and we have only one animation for a *walk* cycle. With the lack of a locomotor system in our virtual character, this is how it would look:

Climbing stair without locomotion

First, we play the walk animation and advance the player forward. Now the character knows it's penetrating the surface. So, the collision detection system pulls the character up above the surface to prevent this penetration. This is how we usually set up the movement on an uneven surface. Even though it doesn't give a realistic look and feel, it does the job and is cheap to implement.

Let's take a look at how we walk upstairs in reality. We put our step firmly on the staircase and using this force, we pull up the rest of our body for the next step. This is how we do it in real life with our advanced locomotor system. However, it's not so simple to implement this level of realism inside games. We'll need a lot of animations for different scenarios, which include climbing ladders, walking/running upstairs, and so on. So, only the large studios with a lot of animators could pull this off in the past, until we came up with an automated system:

With a locomotion system

Fortunately, Unity 3D has an extension that can do just that:

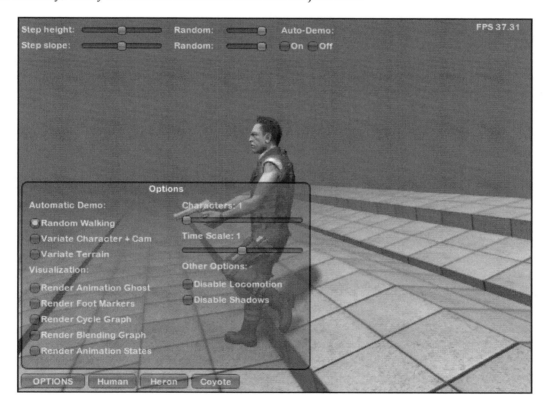

Locomotion system Unity extension

This system can automatically blend our animated walk/run cycles, and adjust the movements of the bones in the legs to ensure that the feet step correctly on the ground. It can also adjust the original animations made for a specific speed and direction on any surface, arbitrary steps, and slopes. We'll see how to use this locomotion system to apply realistic movement to our AI characters in a later chapter.

Summary

Game AI and academic AI have different objectives. Academic AI researchers try to solve real-world problems and develop AI algorithms that have to compete with human intelligence with the ultimate goal of replacing humans in complex situations. Game AI focuses on building NPCs with limited resources that seem to be intelligent to the player with the ultimate goal of entertaining the players. The objective of AI in games is to provide a challenging opponent that makes the game more fun to play. We also learned briefly about the widely used different AI techniques in games, such as FSMs, random and probability, sensor and input system, flocking and group behaviors, path following and steering behaviors, AI pathfinding, navigation mesh generation, and behavior trees. We'll see how to implement these techniques inside the Unity engine in the following chapters. In the next chapter, we will start from the very basic: Finite State Machines.

Finite State Machines

2

In this chapter, we'll learn how to implement a **Finite State Machine (FSM)** in a Unity3D game by studying the simple tank game-mechanic example that comes with this book.

In our game, the player controls a tank. The enemy tanks move around the scene, following four waypoints. Once the player's tank enters the vision range of the enemy tanks, they will start chasing it; then, once they are close enough to attack, they'll start shooting at our player's tank.

To control the AI of our enemy tanks, we use FSM. First, we'll use simple `switch` statements to implement our tank AI states, then we'll use an FSM framework based on and adapted from the C# FSM framework that can be found at `http://wiki.unity3d.com/index.php?title=Finite_State_Machine`.

The topics we will be covering in this chapter are the following:

- The player's tank
- The Bullet class
- Setting up waypoints
- The abstract FSM class
- The enemy tank AI
- Using an FSM framework

The player's tank

Before writing the script for our player's tank, let's take a look at how we set up the **PlayerTank** game object. Our **Tank** object is a simple **Mesh** with the **Rigidbody** and **Box Collider** components. The **Tank** object is composed of two separate meshes, **Tank** and **Turret**, such that **Turret** is a child of **Tank**. This structure allows for the independent rotation of the **Turret** object using the mouse movement and, at the same time, will follow automatically the **Tank** body wherever it goes. Then, we create an empty game object for our **SpawnPoint** transform. We use it as a reference position point when shooting a bullet. Finally, for the player's **Tank**, we need to assign the **Player** tag to our **Tank** object. Now let's take a look at the controller class:

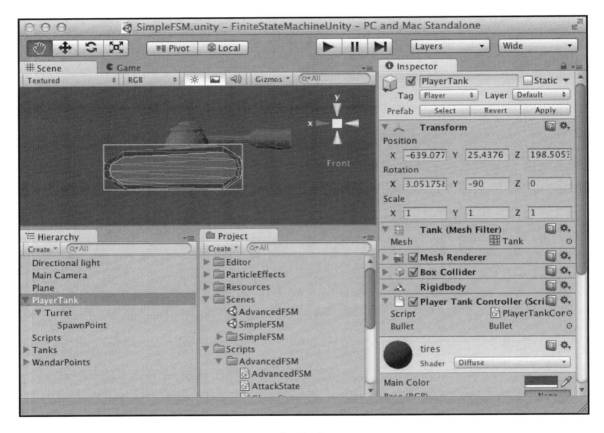

Our tank entity

The player's **Tank** is controlled by the `PlayerTankController` class. We are using the *W*, *A*, *S*, and *D* keys to move and steer the tank, and the left mouse button to aim and shoot from the **Turret** object.

 In this book, we assume the use of a QWERTY keyboard, as well as the use of a two-button mouse, with the left mouse button set to the primary mouse button. For those readers who use a different keyboard, all you have to do is pretend that you are using a QWERTY keyboard or try to modify the code to adapt it to your keyboard layout. It is pretty easy!

Initialization

In the following code, we can see our `TankController` class. First, we set up our `Start` function and the `Update` functions.

The code in the `PlayerTankController.cs` file is as follows:

```
using UnityEngine;
using System.Collections;

public class PlayerTankController : MonoBehaviour
{
    public GameObject Bullet;

    private Transform Turret;
    private Transform bulletSpawnPoint;
    private float curSpeed, targetSpeed, rotSpeed;
    private float turretRotSpeed = 10.0f;
    private float maxForwardSpeed = 300.0f;
    private float maxBackwardSpeed = -300.0f;

    //Bullet shooting rate
    protected float shootRate = 0.5f;
    protected float elapsedTime;

    void Start()
    {

      //Tank Settings
      rotSpeed = 150.0f;

      //Get the turret of the tank
      Turret = gameObject.transform.GetChild(0).transform;
      bulletSpawnPoint = Turret.GetChild(0).transform;
    }
```

```
void Update()
{
  UpdateWeapon();
  UpdateControl();
}
```

The first—and only—child object of our tank entity is the `Turret` object, and the first—and only—child of the `Turret` object is the `bulletSpawnPoint`. The `Start` function finds these objects and then assigns them to their respective variables. Later, after we create the `Bullet` object, we assign it from the **inspector**. Also, we included the `Update` function that calls our `UpdateControl` and `UpdateWeapon` functions, which we will create soon.

Shooting bullet

Whenever the player clicks the left mouse button, we check whether the total elapsed time since the last fire has passed the fire rate of the weapon. If it has, then we create a new `Bullet` object at the `SpawnPoint` variable's position. In this way, we can prevent the player from shooting a continuous stream of bullets:

```
void UpdateWeapon()
{
  if (Input.GetMouseButtonDown(0))
  {
    elapsedTime += Time.deltaTime;
    if (elapsedTime >= shootRate)
    {
      //Reset the time
      elapsedTime = 0.0f;

      //Instantiate the bullet
      Instantiate(Bullet, bulletSpawnPoint.position,
      bulletSpawnPoint.rotation);
    }
  }
}
```

Controlling the tank

The player can rotate the `Turret` object using the mouse. This part may be a little bit tricky because it involves raycasting and 3D rotations. The `Camera` looks down upon the battlefield:

```
void UpdateControl()
{
```

```
//AIMING WITH THE MOUSE
//Generate a plane that intersects the transform's
//position with an upwards normal.
Plane playerPlane = new Plane(Vector3.up,
transform.position + new Vector3(0, 0, 0));

// Generate a ray from the cursor position
Ray RayCast =
Camera.main.ScreenPointToRay(Input.mousePosition);

//Determine the point where the cursor ray intersects
//the plane.
float HitDist = 0;

// If the ray is parallel to the plane, Raycast will
//return false.
if (playerPlane.Raycast(RayCast, out HitDist))
{
  //Get the point along the ray that hits the
  //calculated distance.
  Vector3 RayHitPoint = RayCast.GetPoint(HitDist);

  Quaternion targetRotation =
  Quaternion.LookRotation(RayHitPoint -
  transform.position);

  Turret.transform.rotation =
  Quaternion.Slerp(Turret.transform.rotation,
  targetRotation, Time.deltaTime *
  turretRotSpeed);
}
```

We use raycasting to determine the turning direction by finding the mousePosition coordinates on the battlefield:

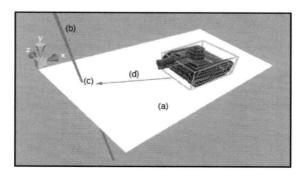

Raycast to aim with the mouse

Raycasting is a tool provided by default in the Unity physics engine. It allows us to find the intersection point between an imaginary line (the ray) and a collider in the scene. Imagine this as a laser pointer: we can fire our laser in a direction and see the point where it hits. However, this is an expensive operation, so try to not exaggerate with the length and number of rays you fire in each frame.

This is how it works:

1. Set up a plane that intersects with the player tank with an upward normal
2. Shoot a ray from screen space with the mouse position (in the preceding diagram, it's assumed that we're looking down at the tank)
3. Find the point where the ray intersects the plane
4. Finally, find the rotation from the current position to that intersection point

Then we check for the key-pressed inputs, and move or rotate the tank accordingly:

```
if (Input.GetKey(KeyCode.W))
{
  targetSpeed = maxForwardSpeed;
}
else if (Input.GetKey(KeyCode.S))
{
  targetSpeed = maxBackwardSpeed;
}
else
{
  targetSpeed = 0;
 }

if (Input.GetKey(KeyCode.A))
{
  transform.Rotate(0, -rotSpeed * Time.deltaTime,
  0.0f);
}
else if (Input.GetKey(KeyCode.D))
{
  transform.Rotate(0, rotSpeed * Time.deltaTime,
  0.0f);
}

//Determine current speed
curSpeed = Mathf.Lerp(curSpeed, targetSpeed, 7.0f *
Time.deltaTime);
transform.Translate(Vector3.forward * Time.deltaTime *
curSpeed);
```

```
        }
    }
```

The Bullet class

Next, we set up our **Bullet** prefab with two orthogonal planes using a laser-like material and a **Particles/Additive** property in the **Shader** field:

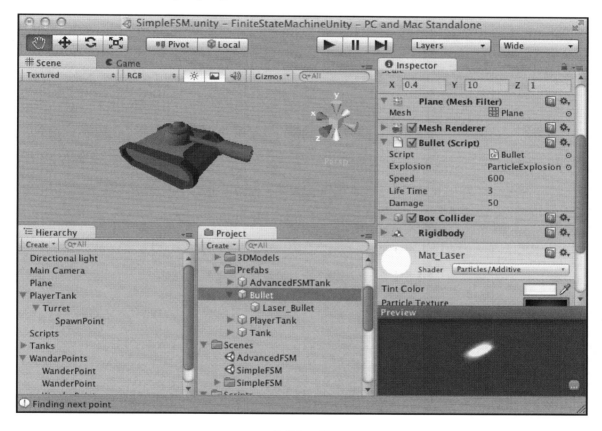

Our Bullet prefab

The code in the `Bullet.cs` file is as follows:

```
using UnityEngine;
using System.Collections;

public class Bullet : MonoBehaviour
```

```
{
    //Explosion Effect
    [SerializeField]
    private GameObject Explosion;
    [SerializeField]
    private float Speed = 600.0f;
    [SerializeField]
    private float LifeTime = 3.0f;
    public int damage = 50;

    void Start()
    {
        Destroy(gameObject, LifeTime);
    }

    void Update()
    {
        transform.position +=
        transform.forward * Speed * Time.deltaTime;
    }

    void OnCollisionEnter(Collision collision)
    {
        ContactPoint contact = collision.contacts[0];
        Instantiate(Explosion, contact.point,
        Quaternion.identity);
        Destroy(gameObject);
    }
}
```

Our `Bullet` has three properties: `damage`, `Speed`, and `Lifetime`—the latter so that the bullet will be automatically destroyed after a certain amount of time. Note that we use `[SerializeField]` to show the private fields in the inspector; by defult, in fact, Unity only shows public fields. It is a good practice to set as `public` only fields that are used in other classes.

As you can see, the **Explosion** property of the bullet is linked to the **ParticleExplosion** prefab, which we're not going to discuss in detail. There's a prefab called **ParticleExplosion** under the `ParticleEffects` folder. We just drop that prefab into this field. This particle effect is played when the bullet hits something, as described in the `OnCollisionEnter` method. The **ParticleExplosion** prefab uses a script called `AutoDestruct` to destroy the `Explosion` object automatically after a small amount of time.

```
using UnityEngine;

public class AutoDestruct : MonoBehaviour
```

```
{
    [SerializeField]
    private float DestructTime = 2.0f;

    void Start()
    {
        Destroy(gameObject, DestructTime);
    }
}
```

The AutoDestruct is a small but convenient script. It just destroys the attached object after a certain amount of seconds. Unity games use a similar script almost every time for many situations.

Setting up waypoints

Next, we will put four **Cube** game objects at random places. They represent *waypoints* inside our scene and, therefore, we name them **WandarPoints**:

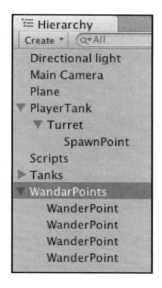

WandarPoints

Here is what our **WandarPoint** object will look like:

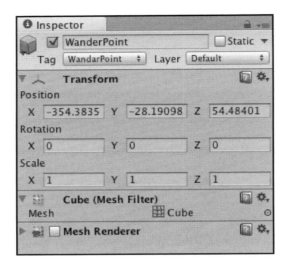

WanderPoint properties

Note that we need to tag those points with a tag called **WandarPoint**. Later, we use this tag when we try to find the waypoints from our tank AI. As you can see in its properties, a waypoint is just a **Cube** game object with the **Mesh Renderer** checkbox disabled, and the **Box Collider** object removed.

We can select the gizmo icon by clicking the small arrow near the object's name in the inspector

We could even use an empty object with a gizmo icon since all we need from a waypoint is its position and the transformation data. However, we're using the **Cube** objects here so that waypoints are easier to visualize.

The abstract FSM class

Next, we implement a generic abstract class to define the methods that our enemy tank AI class has to implement.

The code in the FSM.cs file is as follows:

```
using UnityEngine;
using System.Collections;

public class FSM : MonoBehaviour
{
    //Player Transform
    protected Transform playerTransform;

    //Next destination position of the NPC Tank
    protected Vector3 destPos;

    //List of points for patrolling
    protected GameObject[] pointList;

    //Bullet shooting rate
    protected float shootRate;
    protected float elapsedTime;

    //Tank Turret
    public Transform turret { get; set; }
    public Transform bulletSpawnPoint { get; set; }

    protected virtual void Initialize() { }
    protected virtual void FSMUpdate() { }
    protected virtual void FSMFixedUpdate() { }

    // Use this for initialization
    void Start ()
    {
      Initialize();
    }
    // Update is called once per frame
    void Update ()
    {
```

```
      FSMUpdate();
   }

   void FixedUpdate()
   {
      FSMFixedUpdate();
   }
}
```

The enemy tanks need only to know the position of the player's tank, their next destination point, and the list of waypoints to choose from while they're patrolling. Once the player tank is in range, they rotate their `turret` object and then start shooting from the bullet spawn point at their fire rate.

The inherited classes will also need to implement the three methods: `Initialize`, `FSMUpdate`, and `FSMFixedUpdate`.

The enemy tank AI

Let's look at the real code for our AI tanks. Let's create a new class, called `SimpleFSM`, which inherits from our `FSM` abstract class.

The code in the `SimpleFSM.cs` file is as follows:

```
using UnityEngine;
using System.Collections;

public class SimpleFSM : FSM
{

    public enum FSMState
    {
      None,
      Patrol,
      Chase,
      Attack,
      Dead,
    }

    //Current state that the NPC is reaching
    public FSMState curState;

    //Speed of the tank
    private float curSpeed;
```

```
//Tank Rotation Speed
private float curRotSpeed;

//Bullet
[SerializeField]
private GameObject Bullet;

//Whether the NPC is destroyed or not
private bool bDead;
private int health;

// We overwrite the deprecated built-in `rigidbody` variable.
new private Rigidbody rigidbody;
```

Here, we declare a few variables. Our tank AI will have four different states: Patrol, Chase, Attack, and Dead. Basically, we are implementing the FSM that we described as an example in Chapter 1, *Introduction to AI*:

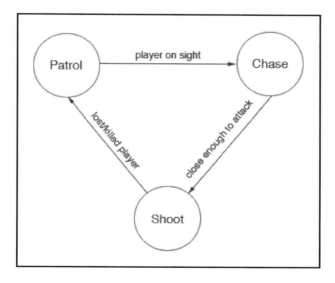

The enemy tank AI's FSM

In our Initialize method, we set up our AI tank's properties with default values. Then we store the positions of waypoints in our local variable. We got those waypoints from our scene using the FindGameObjectsWithTag method, trying to find those objects with the WandarPoint tag:

```
//Initialize the Finite state machine for the NPC tank
protected override void Initialize ()
```

```
{
  curState = FSMState.Patrol;
  curSpeed = 150.0f;
  curRotSpeed = 2.0f;
  bDead = false;
  elapsedTime = 0.0f;
  shootRate = 3.0f;
  health = 100;

  //Get the list of points
  pointList =
  GameObject.FindGameObjectsWithTag("WandarPoint");

  //Set Random destination point first
  FindNextPoint();

  //Get the target enemy(Player)
  GameObject objPlayer =
  GameObject.FindGameObjectWithTag("Player");

  // Get the rigidbody
  rigidbody = GetComponent<Rigidbody>();

  playerTransform = objPlayer.transform;

  if (!playerTransform)
    print("Player doesn't exist.. Please add one "+
    "with Tag named 'Player'");

    //Get the turret of the tank
    turret = gameObject.transform.GetChild(0).transform;
    bulletSpawnPoint = turret.GetChild(0).transform;
}
```

The Update method that gets called every frame looks as follows:

```
//Update each frame
protected override void FSMUpdate()
{
  switch (curState)
  {
    case FSMState.Patrol: UpdatePatrolState(); break;
    case FSMState.Chase: UpdateChaseState(); break;
    case FSMState.Attack: UpdateAttackState(); break;
    case FSMState.Dead: UpdateDeadState(); break;
  }

  //Update the time
```

```
elapsedTime += Time.deltaTime;

//Go to dead state is no health left
if (health <= 0)
  curState = FSMState.Dead;
}
```

We check the current state and then call the appropriate state method. Once the `health` object has a value of zero or less, we set the tank to the `Dead` state.

The Patrol state

While our tank is in the `Patrol` state, we check whether it has reached the destination point. If so, it finds the next destination point to follow. The `FindNextPoint` method basically chooses the next random destination point among the waypoints defined. If it's still on the way to the current destination point, it'll check the distance to the player's tank. If the player's tank is in range (which we choose to be 300 here), then it switches to the `Chase` state. The rest of the code just rotates the tank and moves forward:

```
protected void UpdatePatrolState()
{
  //Find another random patrol point if the current
  //point is reached
  if (Vector3.Distance(transform.position, destPos) <=
  100.0f)
  {
    print("Reached to the destination point\n"+
    "calculating the next point");

    FindNextPoint();
  }

  //Check the distance with player tank
  //When the distance is near, transition to chase state
  else if (Vector3.Distance(transform.position,
  playerTransform.position) <= 300.0f)
  {
    print("Switch to Chase Position");
    curState = FSMState.Chase;
  }

  //Rotate to the target point
  Quaternion targetRotation =
  Quaternion.LookRotation(destPos
  - transform.position);
```

```
      transform.rotation =
      Quaternion.Slerp(transform.rotation,
      targetRotation, Time.deltaTime * curRotSpeed);

      //Go Forward
      transform.Translate(Vector3.forward * Time.deltaTime *
      curSpeed);
}
protected void FindNextPoint()
{
   print("Finding next point");
   int rndIndex = Random.Range(0, pointList.Length);
   float rndRadius = 10.0f;
   Vector3 rndPosition = Vector3.zero;
   destPos = pointList[rndIndex].transform.position +
   rndPosition;

   //Check Range to decide the random point
   //as the same as before
   if (IsInCurrentRange(destPos))
   {
      rndPosition = new Vector3(Random.Range(-rndRadius,
      rndRadius), 0.0f, Random.Range(-rndRadius,
      rndRadius));
      destPos = pointList[rndIndex].transform.position +
      rndPosition;
   }
}
protected bool IsInCurrentRange(Vector3 pos)
{
   float xPos = Mathf.Abs(pos.x - transform.position.x);
   float zPos = Mathf.Abs(pos.z - transform.position.z);

   if (xPos <= 50 && zPos <= 50)
      return true;

      return false;
}
```

The Chase state

Similarly, while the tank is in the Chase state, it checks its distance with the player tank. If it's close enough, it'll switch to the Attack state. If the player tank has gone too far, then it'll go back to the Patrol state:

```
protected void UpdateChaseState()
{
  //Set the target position as the player position
  destPos = playerTransform.position;

  //Check the distance with player tank When
  //the distance is near, transition to attack state
  float dist = Vector3.Distance(transform.position,
  playerTransform.position);

  if (dist <= 200.0f)
  {
    curState = FSMState.Attack;
  }
  //Go back to patrol is it become too far
  else if (dist >= 300.0f)
  {
    curState = FSMState.Patrol;
  }

  //Go Forward
  transform.Translate(Vector3.forward * Time.deltaTime *
  curSpeed);
}
```

The Attack state

If the player tank is close enough to attack our AI tank, we will rotate the turret object to face the player tank, and then start shooting. Then, if the player tank goes out of range, the tank goes back to the Patrol state:

```
protected void UpdateAttackState()
{
  //Set the target position as the player position
  destPos = playerTransform.position;

  //Check the distance with the player tank
  float dist = Vector3.Distance(transform.position,
  playerTransform.position);
```

```
if (dist >= 200.0f && dist < 300.0f)
{
  //Rotate to the target point
  Quaternion targetRotation =
  Quaternion.LookRotation(destPos -
  transform.position);
  transform.rotation = Quaternion.Slerp(
  transform.rotation, targetRotation,
  Time.deltaTime * curRotSpeed);

  //Go Forward
  transform.Translate(Vector3.forward *
  Time.deltaTime * curSpeed);

  curState = FSMState.Attack;
}
//Transition to patrol is the tank become too far
else if (dist >= 300.0f)
{
  curState = FSMState.Patrol;
}

//Always turn the turret toward the player
Quaternion turretRotation =
Quaternion.LookRotation(destPos
- turret.position);

turret.rotation =
Quaternion.Slerp(turret.rotation, turretRotation,
Time.deltaTime * curRotSpeed);

//Shoot the bullets
ShootBullet();
}
private void ShootBullet()
{
  if (elapsedTime >= shootRate)
  {
    //Shoot the bullet
    Instantiate(Bullet, bulletSpawnPoint.position,
    bulletSpawnPoint.rotation);
    elapsedTime = 0.0f;
  }
}
```

The Dead state

If the tank has reached the Dead state, we make it explode:

```
protected void UpdateDeadState()
{
  //Show the dead animation with some physics effects
  if (!bDead)
  {
    bDead = true;
    Explode();
  }
}
```

Here's a small function that will give a nice explosion effect. We just apply an ExplosionForce function to our rigidbody component with some random directions, as shown in the following code:

```
protected void Explode()
{
  float rndX = Random.Range(10.0f, 30.0f);
  float rndZ = Random.Range(10.0f, 30.0f);
  for (int i = 0; i < 3; i++)
  {
    rigidbody.AddExplosionForce(10000.0f,
    transform.position - new Vector3(rndX, 10.0f,
    rndZ), 40.0f, 10.0f);
    rigidbody.velocity = transform.TransformDirection(
    new Vector3(rndX, 20.0f, rndZ));
  }

  Destroy(gameObject, 1.5f);
}
```

Taking damage

If the tank is hit by a bullet, then the health property's value will be decreased according to the Bullet object's damage value:

```
void OnCollisionEnter(Collision collision)
{
  //Reduce health
  if(collision.gameObject.tag == "Bullet")
  {
    health -=collision.gameObject.GetComponent
    <Bullet>().damage;
```

```
        }
    }
```

You can open the `SimpleFSM.scene` file in Unity; you should see the AI tanks patrolling, chasing, and attacking the player. Our player's tank doesn't take damage from AI tanks yet, so it never gets destroyed. But AI tanks have the `health` property and take damage from the player's bullets, so you'll see them explode once their `health` property reaches zero:

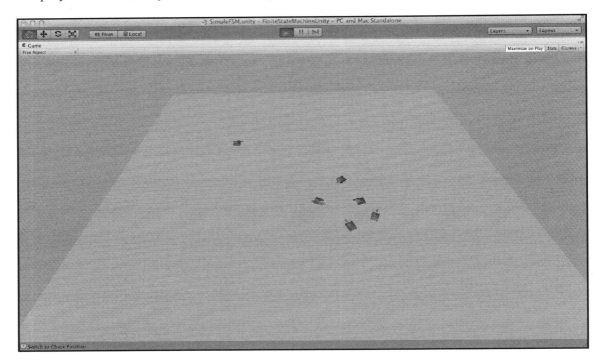

The AI tanks in action

Using an FSM framework

The FSM framework we're going to use here is adapted from the C# FSM framework, which can be found at https://wiki.unity3d.com/index.php?title=Finite_State_Machine. That framework is again a part of the Deterministic Finite State Machine framework, based on *Chapter 3.1* of *Game Programming Gems 1*, by Eric Dybsend. We'll only be looking at the differences between this FSM and the one we made earlier. The complete FSM can be found with the assets that come with the book. We'll now study how the framework works and how we can use it to implement our tank AI.

AdvanceFSM and FSMState are the two main classes of our framework. Let's take a look at them first.

The AdvanceFSM class

The AdvanceFSM class basically manages all the FSMState classes we've implemented, and keeps updated with the transitions and the current state. So, the first thing to do before using our framework is to declare the transitions and states that we plan to implement for our AI tanks.

The code in the AdvancedFSM.cs file is as follows:

```
using UnityEngine;
using System.Collections;
using System.Collections.Generic;

public enum Transition
{
    None = 0,
    SawPlayer,
    ReachPlayer,
    LostPlayer,
    NoHealth,
}

public enum FSMStateID
{
    None = 0,
    Patrolling,
    Chasing,
    Attacking,
    Dead,
}
```

It has a list object to store the FSMState objects, and two local variables to store the current ID of the FSMState class and current FSMState itself.

The AddFSMState and the DeleteState methods add and delete the instances of our FSMState class in our list respectively. When the PerformTransition method is called, it updates the CurrentState variable with the new state according to the transition:

```
private List<FSMState> fsmStates;
    private FSMStateID currentStateID;
    public FSMStateID CurrentStateID
    {
```

```
       get
       {
          return currentStateID;
       }
   }
   private FSMState currentState;
   public FSMState CurrentState
   {
      get
      {
         return currentState;
      }
   }
```

The FSMState class

FSMState manages the transitions to other states. It has a dictionary object called map, which is used to store the key-value pairs of transitions and states. For example, the SawPlayer transition maps to the Chasing state, LostPlayer maps to the Patrolling state, and so on.

The code in the FSMState.cs file is as follows:

```
using UnityEngine;
using System.Collections;
using System.Collections.Generic;

public abstract class FSMState
{
    protected Dictionary<Transition, FSMStateID> map = new
    Dictionary<Transition, FSMStateID>();
...
```

The AddTransition and DeleteTransition methods add and delete transitions from its state-transition dictionary map object. The GetOutputState method looks up from the map object and returns the state based on the input transition.

The FSMState class also declares two abstract methods that its child classes need to implement. They are as follows:

```
...
public abstract void Reason(Transform player, Transform npc);
public abstract void Act(Transform player, Transform npc);
...
```

The `Reason` method has to check whether the state should carry out the transition to another state. The `Act` method, instead, does the actual execution of the tasks for the `currentState` variable, such as moving toward a destination point and chasing or attacking the player. Both methods require transformed data from the player and the NPC entity, which can be obtained using this class.

The state classes

Unlike in our previous `SimpleFSM` example, the states for our tank AI are written in separate classes inherited from the `FSMState` class, such as `AttackState`, `ChaseState`, `DeadState`, and `PatrolState`, each of which implements the `Reason` and `Act` methods. Let's take a look at the `PatrolState` class as an example.

The PatrolState class

This class has three methods: a constructor, a `Reason`, and an `Act`.

The code in the `PatrolState.cs` file is as follows:

```
using UnityEngine;
using System.Collections;

public class PatrolState : FSMState
{

    public PatrolState(Transform[] wp)
    {
      waypoints = wp;
      stateID = FSMStateID.Patrolling;

      curRotSpeed = 1.0f;
      curSpeed = 100.0f;
    }

    public override void Reason(Transform player,
    Transform npc)
    {
      //Check the distance with player tank
      //When the distance is near, transition to chase state
      if (Vector3.Distance(npc.position, player.position) <=
      300.0f)
      {
        Debug.Log("Switch to Chase State");
```

```
        npc.GetComponent
        <NPCTankController>().SetTransition(
        Transition.SawPlayer);
    }
}

public override void Act(Transform player, Transform npc)
{
  //Find another random patrol point if the current
  //point is reached

  if (Vector3.Distance(npc.position, destPos) <= 100.0f)
  {
    Debug.Log("Reached to the destination" +
    point\ncalculating the next point");
    FindNextPoint();
  }

  //Rotate to the target point
  Quaternion targetRotation =
  Quaternion.LookRotation(destPos - npc.position);

  npc.rotation = Quaternion.Slerp(npc.rotation,
  targetRotation, Time.deltaTime * curRotSpeed);

  //Go Forward
  npc.Translate(Vector3.forward *
  Time.deltaTime * curSpeed);
}
}
```

The constructor method takes the waypoints array and stores them in a local array, and then initializes properties such as movement and rotation speed. The Reason method checks the distance between itself (the AI tank) and the player tank. If the player tank is in range, it sets the transition ID to the SawPlayer transition using the SetTransition method of the NPCTankController class, which looks as follows:

```
public void SetTransition(Transition t)
{
    PerformTransition(t);
}
```

This is just a wrapper method that calls the `PerformTransition` method of the `AdvanceFSM` class. This method updates the `CurrentState` variable with the one responsible for this transition, using the `Transition` object and the state-transition dictionary `map` object from the `FSMState` class. The `Act` method updates the AI tank's destination point, rotates the tank in that direction, and then moves forward. Other state classes also follow this template with different reasoning and acting procedures. We've already seen them in our previous simple FSM examples, so we won't describe them here again. See if you can figure out how to set up these classes on your own. If you get stuck, the assets that come with this book contain the code for you to look at.

The NPCTankController class

For the tank AI, the `NPCTankController` class will inherit from `AdvanceFSM`. This is how we set up the states for our NPC tanks:

```
    ...
    private void ConstructFSM()
    {

        PatrolState patrol = new PatrolState(waypoints);
        patrol.AddTransition(Transition.SawPlayer,
        FSMStateID.Chasing);
        patrol.AddTransition(Transition.NoHealth,
        FSMStateID.Dead);

        ChaseState chase = new ChaseState(waypoints);
        chase.AddTransition(Transition.LostPlayer,
        FSMStateID.Patrolling);
        chase.AddTransition(Transition.ReachPlayer,
        FSMStateID.Attacking);
        chase.AddTransition(Transition.NoHealth,
        FSMStateID.Dead);

        AttackState attack = new AttackState(waypoints);
        attack.AddTransition(Transition.LostPlayer,
        FSMStateID.Patrolling);
        attack.AddTransition(Transition.SawPlayer,
        FSMStateID.Chasing);
        attack.AddTransition(Transition.NoHealth,
        FSMStateID.Dead);

        DeadState dead = new DeadState();
        dead.AddTransition(Transition.NoHealth,
        FSMStateID.Dead);
```

```
        AddFSMState(patrol);
        AddFSMState(chase);
        AddFSMState(attack);
        AddFSMState(dead);
    }
```

Here's the beauty of using our FSM framework: since the states are self-managed within their respective classes, our NPCTankController class only needs to call the Reason and Act methods of the currently active state. This fact eliminates the need to write a long list of the if/else and switch statements, and therefore bloat the code. Instead, our states are now nicely packaged in classes of their own, which will make the code more manageable as the number of states and transitions between them grow more and more in larger projects:

```
...
    protected override void FSMFixedUpdate()
    {
        CurrentState.Reason(playerTransform, transform);
        CurrentState.Act(playerTransform, transform);
    }
```

However, the main steps to use this framework can be summarized as follows:

1. Declare transitions and states in the AdvanceFSM class
2. Write the state classes inherited from the FSMState class, and then implement the Reason and Act methods
3. Write the custom NPC AI class inherited from AdvanceFSM
4. Create states from the state classes, and then add transition and state pairs using the AddTransition method of the FSMState class
5. Add those states into the state list of the AdvanceFSM class, using the AddFSMState method
6. Call the CurrentState variable's Reason and Act methods in the game update cycle

You can play around with the AdvancedFSM.scene in Unity. It'll run in the same way as our previous SimpleFSM example, but the code is now more organized and manageable.

Summary

In this chapter, we learned how to implement state machines in Unity3D based on a simple tank game. We first looked at how to implement FSM in the most direct way by using the `switch` statements. Then we studied how to use a framework to make the AI implementation easier to manage and extend.

In the next chapter, we will take a look at randomness and probability, and see how we can use it to make the outcome of our games more unpredictable.

Randomness and Probability 3

In this chapter, we are going to look at how we can apply the concepts of probability and randomness to game AI. This chapter is more about generic game AI development techniques in the areas of randomness and probability, and less about Unity3D in particular. This means that we can apply the concepts of this chapter to any game development middleware or technology framework. We'll be using mono C# in Unity3D for the demos mainly using the console to output data, and won't address much on the specific features of the Unity3D engine and the editor itself.

Game developers use probability to add a little uncertainty to the behaviors of AI characters, as well as to the wider game world. Randomness makes the artificial intelligence system less predictable and provides a more exciting, challenging, and fair experience.

In this chapter, we will look at the following topics:

- We take look at randomness and probability.
- We will be creating a simple dice game. We will also give some examples of applications for probability and dynamic AI.
- We will finish the chapter with a simple demo slot machine.

Randomness in games

Game designers and developers use randomness in game AI to make the game and characters more realistic and varied by not making the same decision or taking the same action again and again.

Let's take an example of a typical soccer game. One of the rules of a soccer game is to award a direct free kick if one player commits a foul while trying to possess the ball from the opposing team. Now, instead of giving a foul and a free kick all the time whenever that foul happens, the game developer can apply a probability so that the game rewards with a direct freekick only 98 percent of all the fouls. As a result, most of the time, the player gets a direct freekick; but when that remaining two percent happens, it can provide emotional feedback to the players from both the teams (assuming that you are playing against another human). The other player would feel angry and disappointed, while you'd feel lucky and satisfied. After all, the referees are human, and like all other humans, they might not be 100 percent correct all the time.

But how can a computer produce random values? And how can we use them in Unity?

Randomness in computer science

Computers are deterministic machines: by design, if we give a computer the same input multiple times, in the form of program code and data, then it returns the same output. Therefore, how can we have a program return unpredictable and random outputs?

If we need *truly random* numbers, then we need to take this randomness from somewhere else. That's why many advanced applications try to combine different external sources of randomness into a random value: they may look at the movement of the mouse in a certain interval, to the noise of the internet connection, or even ask the user to smash the keyboard randomly, and so on. There is even dedicated hardware for random number generation!

Fortunately, in games, we do not need such *truly random* numbers, and can use simpler algorithms that can generate sequences that *look like* a sequence of random numbers. Such algorithms are called **Pseudorandom Number Generators** (**PRNG**): using an initial seed, they can generate, in a deterministic way, a sequence of numbers that statistically approximate the properties of a sequence of truly random numbers. The catch is that, if we start from the same seed, we always get the same sequence of numbers. For this reason, we usually initialize the seed value from something that we imagine is always different every time the user open the application. For instance, the elapsed time in milliseconds since the computer started running, or the number of milliseconds since 1970 (the Unix timestamp). Note, however, that having the possibility to obtain the same random sequence every time is really helpful when debugging!

Finally, note that some PRNGs are more *random* than others. If we were creating an encryption program, we would want to look into less predictable PRNGs, called **Cryptographically Secure Pseudo-Random Number Generator (CSPRNG)**. Fortunately, for games, the simple RNG that comes with Unity is good enough.

The Unity Random class

The Unity3D script has a `Random` class to generate random data. You can set the generator seed using the `InitState(int seed)` function. Usually, we wouldn't want to seed the same value again and again, as this will result in the same predictable sequence of random numbers being generated. One of the reasons for keeping the same seed value is for testing purposes, or if you want your players to be able to generate a procedural map/level with a specific seed.

Then, you can read the `Random.value` property to get a random number between `0.0` and `1.0`. This generator is inclusive, so both `0.0` and `1.0` may be returned by this property.

Another class method that could be quite handy is the `Range` method:

```
static function Range (min : float, max : float) : float
```

The `Range` method can be used to generate a random number from a range. When given an integer value, it returns a random integer number between `min` (inclusive) and `max` (exclusive). This means that a `min` may be returned, but never `max`. If you pass in float values for the range, it'll return a random `float` number between `min` (inclusive) and `max` (exclusive). Take note whenever a parameter is exclusive or inclusive: since the integer random value is exclusive of `max` in range, we'll need to pass in *n+1* as the `max` range if we want *n* to be our desired maximum random integer. On the contrary, for the `float` random value, the `max` value in the range is inclusive.

Simple random dice game

Let's set up a very simple dice game in a new scene where a random number between 1 and 6 is generated, and checked against the input value. The player wins if the input value matches the dice result generated randomly, as shown in the following DiceGame.cs file:

```
public class DiceGame : MonoBehaviour {
  public string inputValue = "1";

    public Text outputText;
    public InputField inputField;
    public Button button;

    int throwNormalDice() {
    Debug.Log("Throwing dice...");
    Debug.Log("Finding random between 1 to 6...");
    int diceResult = Random.Range(1,7);
    Debug.Log("Result: " + diceResult);
    return diceResult;
  }
  int throwLoadedDice() {
    Debug.Log("Throwing dice...");
    int randomProbability = Random.Range(1,101);
    int diceResult = 0;
    if (randomProbability < 36) {
      diceResult = 6;
    }
    else {
      diceResult = Random.Range(1,5);
    }
    Debug.Log("Result: " + diceResult);
    return diceResult;
  }

    public void processGame()
    {
        inputValue = inputField.text;
        try
        {
            int inputInteger = int.Parse(inputValue);
            int totalSix = 0;
            for (var i = 0; i < 10; i++)
            {
                var diceResult = throwNormalDice();
                if (diceResult == 6) { totalSix++; }
```

```
            if (diceResult == inputInteger)
            {
                    outputText.text = "DICE RESULT: " +
diceResult.ToString() + "\r\nYOU WIN!";
            }
            else
            {
                    outputText.text = "DICE RESULT: " +
diceResult.ToString() + "\r\nYOU LOSE!";
            }
        }
        Debug.Log("Total of six: " + totalSix.ToString());
    } catch
    {
        outputText.text = "Input is not a number!";
        Debug.LogError("Input is not a number!");
    }
  }
}
```

We implement this simple dice game in the `DiceGame` class. The `guiText` object is used to display the result. First, we set up the scene: we need to create a `guiText` for the result (navigate to **Game Object | UI | Text**), an input field (**Game Object | UI | Input Field**), and a button (**Game Object | UI |Button**). In the following screenshot, you can see the result of our simple user interface. It is minimal, but functional:

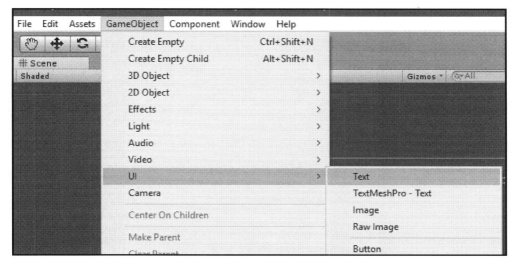

Our simple Unity interface

Then, we create an empty object and attach the script, taking care to connect all the missing reference with the UI elements we created before:

Simple dice game results

Definitions of probability

There are many ways to define probability, based on a given situation and the type of game or application you are building. The most commonly used definition of probability is to consider the probability of an event as the frequency with which the event occurs when we repeat the observation an infinite amount of times. In other words, if we throw a die 100 times, we expect to see a six, on average, 1/6th of the times, and we should get closer and closer to 1/6th with 1,000/10,000/one million throws.

We can write the probability for an event A to occur as P(A). To calculate P(A) we need to know all the possible outcomes (N) for the observation and the total number of times in which the desired event occurs (n).

So, the probability of an event A can be calculated as the following:

$$P(A) = \frac{n}{N}$$

If P(A) is the probability of the event A to successfully occur, then the probability of the event A will not occur is equal to the following:

$$\bar{P}(A) = 1 - P(A)$$

The probability must be a real number between zero and one. Having a probability of zero means there's no chance for the desired event to occur; on the other hand, having a probability of one means that the event will occur for sure. As a consequence, the following must equal to one:

$$P(A) + \bar{P}(A)$$

Independent and related events

Another important concept in probability is whether the chance of a particular event occurring depends on any other event in some way. For example, consider the event *throwing a six-sided die twice and getting a double 6*. Each dice throw can be considered an independent event. Each time you throw a die, the probability of each side turning up is one in six, and the outcome of the second dice roll will not change depending on the result of the first roll. On the other hand, in the event *drawing two aces from the same deck*, each draw is not independent of the others. If you drew an ace in the first event, the probability of getting another ace the second time is different, because now there is one less ace in the deck.

Independence of events is important because it allows us to significantly simplify some calculations. For instance, imagine that we want to know the probability of the event *either event* **A** or *event* **B** *will happen*. If **A** and **B** are two independent events, then we can just sum the probabilities of **A** and **B**:

$$P(A \text{ or } B) = P(A) + P(B)$$

In the same way, if we have an event *both event* **A** and **B** *will happen*, then we can just multiply the individual probabilities together:

$$P(A \text{ and } B) = P(A) \cdot P(B)$$

For instance, if we want to know the probability of getting two sixes by throwing two dice, we can just multiply 1/6 by 1/6 and get the correct probability: 1/36.

Conditional probability

Now, let's consider another example. We are still throwing two dice, but this time, we are interested in the probability that the *sum* of the numbers showing up on two dice is equal to two. Since there's only one way to get this sum, which is one and one, the probability is the same as getting the same number on both dice. In that case, it would still be 1/36.

But how about getting the sum of the numbers that show up on the two dice to seven? As you can see, there are a total of six possible ways of getting a total of seven, outlined in the following table:

Dice 1	Dice 2
1	6
2	5
3	4
4	3
5	2
6	1

In this case, we need to use the general probability formula. From the preceding table, we can see that we have six outcomes that give us a total sum of seven. Because we know that there are 36 total possible outcomes for two dice, we can easily compute the final probability as 6/36 or one-sixth (which is 16.7%).

Loaded dice

Now, let's assume that we haven't been all too honest, and our dice are loaded so that the side of the number six has a double chance of landing facing upward. Since we doubled the chance of getting six, we need to double the probability of getting six, let's say, up to roughly one third (0.34), and, as a consequence, the rest will be equally spread over the remaining five sides (0.132 each).

We can implement a loaded dice algorithm in this way: first, we generate a random value between 1 and 100. Then, we check if the random value falls between 1 and 35. If so, our algorithm returns 6; otherwise, we get a random dice value between one and five, since these values have the same probability.

So, here's our `throwLoadedDice()` method:

```
int throwDiceLoaded() {
  Debug.Log("Throwing dice...");
    int randomProbability = Random.Range(1,101);
    int diceResult = 0;
    if (randomProbability < 36) {
      diceResult = 6;
    }
    else {
      diceResult = Random.Range(1,5);
    }
  Debug.Log("Result: " + diceResult);
    return diceResult;
}
```

If we test our new loaded dice algorithm by throwing the dice multiple times, you'll notice that the value 6 yields more than usual. To do that, just swap the dice throwing function in the `processGame()` function:

```
public void processGame()
{
    inputValue = inputField.text;
    try
    {
        int inputInteger = int.Parse(inputValue);
        int totalSix = 0;
        for (var i = 0; i < 10; i++)
        {
            var diceResult = throwLoadedDice();
            if (diceResult == 6) { totalSix++; }

            if (diceResult == inputInteger)
            {
                outputText.text = "DICE RESULT: " +
diceResult.ToString() + "\r\nYOU WIN!";
            }
            else
            {
                outputText.text = "DICE RESULT: " +
diceResult.ToString() + "\r\nYOU LOSE!";
            }
        }
        Debug.Log("Total of six: " + totalSix.ToString());
    } catch
    {
        outputText.text = "Input is not a number!";
```

```
                    Debug.LogError("Input is not a number!");
        }
    }
```

As you can see, the code is identical to the previous example. This time, however, we are throwing an *unfair* dice that returns six much more than it should. Remember, in game design, it's not cheating if the goal is to give the player a more exciting and fun experience!

Character personalities

Probability and randomness are not only about dice. We can also use a probability distribution to specify the in-game character's specialties. Let's pretend we designed a game proposal for a population management game for the local government. We need to address and simulate issues such as taxation versus global talent attraction, immigration versus social cohesion, and so on. We have three types of characters in our proposal; namely, workers, scientists, and professionals. Their efficiencies in performing their particular tasks are defined in the following table:

Characters	Construction	R&D	Corporate jobs
Worker	95	2	3
Scientist	5	85	10
Professional	10	10	80

Let's take a look at how we can implement this scenario. Let's say the player needs to build new houses to accommodate the increased population. A house construction would require 1,000 units of workload to finish. We use the value specified earlier as the workload that can be done per second per unit type for a particular task. So if you're building a house with one worker, it'll only take about 10 seconds to finish the construction (1000/95), whereas it'll take more than three minutes if you are trying to build with the scientists (1000/5 = 200 seconds). The same will be true for other tasks, such as **Research and Development (R&D)** and corporate jobs. These factors can be adjusted or enhanced later as the game progresses, making some of the entry-level tasks become simpler, and takes less time.

Then we introduce special items that could be discovered by the particular unit type. We don't want to give out these items every time a particular unit has done its tasks. Instead, we want to reward the player as a surprise. So, we associate the probability of finding such items according to the unit type, as described in the following table:

Special items	Worker	Scientist	Professional
Raw materials	0.3	0.1	0.0
New tech	0.0	0.3	0.0
Bonus	0.1	0.2	0.4

The preceding table shows there's a 30 percent chance that a worker will find some raw materials, and a 10 percent chance to earn bonus income whenever they have built a factory or a house. This allows the players to anticipate possible upcoming rewards once they've done some tasks, and can make the game more fun because the players will not know the outcome of the event.

FSM with probability

We discussed FSM in `Chapter 2`, *Finite State Machines*, using both simple switch statements and the FSM framework. The decision to choose which state to execute was purely based on the true or false value of a given condition. Cast your mind back to the following FSM of our AI-controlled tank entity:

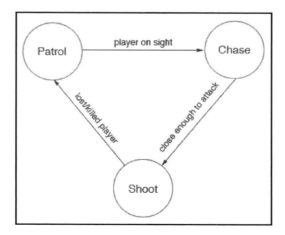

Tank AI FSM

To make the AI more interesting, and a little bit unpredictable, we can give our tank entity some options to choose from, instead of doing the same thing whenever a certain condition is met. For example, in our earlier FSM, our AI tank would always chase the player tank once the player was in its line of sight. Instead, we can split the **player on sight** transaction in order to connect a new state, **Flee**. How can the AI decide which state to move to? Randomly, of course:

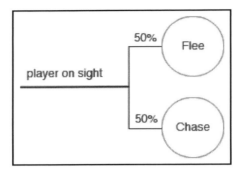

FSM using probability

As shown in the preceding diagram, instead of chasing every time, now, the AI tank spots the player, and there's a 50 percent chance that it'll flee, and maybe report to the headquarters or something. We can implement this mechanism the same way we did with our previous dice example. First, we need to generate a random value between 1 and 100, and see if the value lies between 1 and 50, or 51 and 100. If it's the former, the tank will flee; otherwise, it will chase the player.

Another way to implement this is to fill an array with these options in proportion to their respective probabilities. Then, pick a random state from this pool as if you were drawing a lottery winner. Let's see how we can use this technique, as shown in the following FSM.cs file:

```
using UnityEngine;
using System.Collections;

public class FSM : MonoBehaviour {
  public enum FSMState
    {
        Chase,
        Flee
    }
```

```
public int chaseProbabiilty = 80;
public int fleeProbabiilty = 20;
public ArrayList statesPoll = new ArrayList();
// Use this for initialization
void Start () {
  //fill the array
  for (int i = 0; i < chaseProbabiilty; i++) {
    statesPoll.Add(FSMState.Chase);
  }
  for (int i = 0; i < fleeProbabiilty; i++) {
    statesPoll.Add(FSMState.Flee);
  }
}
// Update is called once per frame
void Update () {
    if (Input.GetKeyDown(KeyCode.Space))
    {
        int randomState = Random.Range(0, statesPoll.Count);
        Debug.Log(statesPoll[randomState].ToString());
    }
  }
}
```

In our `Update()` method, when you press the spacebar, we just choose one random item from our `statesPoll` array. Obviously, the one with more entries in the poll will have a higher chance of being selected.

Note that this solution is more memory-expensive, because we need to store hundreds of items in an array; therefore, it is not advised if we want to run this script on a lot of agents.

Dynamic AI

We can also use probability to specify the intelligence levels of AI characters or the global game settings. This can, in turn, affect the overall difficulty level of the game and keep it challenging and interesting for the players. As described in the book, *The Art of Game Design*, Jesse Schell, Morgan Kaufmann publications, players will only continue to play our game if we keep them in their flow channel:

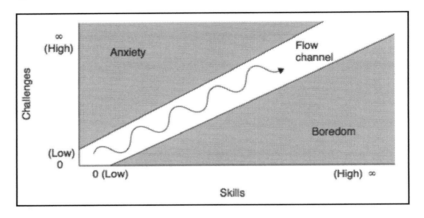

The player's flow channel

The players feel anxious and get disappointed if we present tough challenges for them before they have the necessary skills. On the other hand, once they've mastered the skills, if we continue to keep the game at the same pace, they will get bored. The area in which the players are kept engaged for a long time is in between these two extremes of hard and easy, which the original author referred to as the flow channel. To keep the players in the flow channel, the game designers need to feed the challenges and missions that match with the progressive skills that the players have acquired over time. However, it is not an easy task to find a value that works for all players, since the pace of learning and the expectations can be different from individual to individual.

One way to tackle this problem is to collect the player's attempts and results during the gameplay sessions, and to adjust the difficulty of the opponent's AI accordingly. How can we change AI's difficulty? For instance, by making the AI more aggressive, increasing the probability of landing a perfect shot, or decreasing the probability of erratic behavior.

Though this approach is supposed to create more engaging games, there are many players who don't like this approach, since it takes away the pride and satisfaction of finishing a hard game. After all, beating a very hard boss AI character despite all the challenges can be much more rewarding and satisfying than winning the game because the AI is dumb. They would feel much worse if they found out that the AI becomes dumber and dumber the more they fail to beat a boss. Therefore, we'll need to be careful about when we apply this technique in our games.

Demo slot machine

In this final demo, we'll design and implement a slot machine game with 10 symbols and three reels. To make it simple, we'll use the numbers from 0 to 9 as our symbols. Many slot machines would use fruit shapes and other simple shapes, such as bells, stars, and letters. Some other slot machines usually use a specific theme, based on popular movies or TV franchises. Since there are 10 symbols and 3 reels, that's a total of 1,000 (10^3) possible combinations.

Random slot machine

This random slot machine demo is similar to our previous dice example. This time, we are going to generate three random numbers for three reels. The only payout will be when you get three of the same symbols on the payline. To make it simpler, we'll only have one line to play against in this demo. If the player wins, the game will return 500 times the bet amount.

We'll set up our scene with all our UI elements: three texts for the reels, another text element for the YOU WIN or YOU LOSE text, one text element for the player's credits, an input field for the bet, and a button to *pull the lever*.

Our GUI text objects

This is how our new script looks, as shown in the following `SlotMachine.cs` file:

```
using UnityEngine;
using UnityEngine.UI;

public class SlotMachine : MonoBehaviour {
  public float spinDuration = 2.0f;
  public int numberOfSym = 10;

  public Text firstReel;
  public Text secondReel;
  public Text thirdReel;
  public Text betResult;

  public Text totalCredits;
  public InputField inputBet;
  private bool startSpin = false;
  private bool firstReelSpinned = false;
  private bool secondReelSpinned = false;
  private bool thirdReelSpinned = false;
  private int betAmount;
  private int credits = 1000;
  private int firstReelResult = 0;
  private int secondReelResult = 0;
  private int thirdReelResult = 0;
  private float elapsedTime = 0.0f;
```

First, we start by listing all the class attributes we need. Again, note it is a good programming practice to avoid public fields, unless strictly necessary. Therefore, you should use the [SerializeField] attribute instead. Here, however, we use the public attribute to avoid making the code listing too long. Now, let's continue:

```
public void Spin()
  {
      if (betAmount > 0)
      {
          startSpin = true;
      } else
      {
          betResult.text = "Insert a valid bet!";
      }
  }

  private void OnGUI()
  {
      try
      {
```

```
        betAmount = int.Parse(inputBet.text);
    }
    catch
    {
        betAmount = 0;
    }
    totalCredits.text = credits.ToString();
}

void checkBet() {
    if (firstReelResult == secondReelResult && secondReelResult ==
thirdReelResult) {
        betResult.text = "YOU WIN!";
            credits += 500*betAmount;
    }
    else {
        betResult.text = "YOU LOSE!";
            credits -= betAmount;
    }
}
```

We create some basic functions like Spin, that starts the slot machine, the OnGui function, that update the user interface, and checkBet, that checks if the player won or not.

```
void FixedUpdate () {
    if (startSpin) {
        elapsedTime += Time.deltaTime;
        int randomSpinResult = Random.Range(0, numberOfSym);
        if (!firstReelSpinned) {
            firstReel.text = randomSpinResult.ToString();
            if (elapsedTime >= spinDuration) {
                firstReelResult = randomSpinResult;
                firstReelSpinned = true;
                elapsedTime = 0;
            }
        }
        else if (!secondReelSpinned) {
            secondReel.text = randomSpinResult.ToString();
            if (elapsedTime >= spinDuration) {
                secondReelResult = randomSpinResult;
                secondReelSpinned = true;
                elapsedTime = 0;
            }
        }
        else if (!thirdReelSpinned) {
            thirdReel.text = randomSpinResult.ToString();
            if (elapsedTime >= spinDuration) {
                thirdReelResult = randomSpinResult;
```

```
            startSpin = false;
            elapsedTime = 0;
            firstReelSpinned = false;
            secondReelSpinned = false;
            checkBet();
        }
      }
    }
  }
}
```

Attach the script to an empty `GameController` object and then fill in the referenced object in the inspector. Then, we need to connect the `Button` to the `Spin()` method. To do that, select the `Button` and fill the **On Click()** event handler in the inspector, as shown in the following screenshot:

When we click the button, we will set the `startSpin` flag to true. Once spinning, in our `FixedUpdate()` method, we generate a random value for each reel. Finally, once we've got the value for the third reel, we reset the `startSpin` flag to false. While we are getting the random value for each reel, we also keep track of how much time has elapsed since the player pulled the lever. Usually, in the real world slot machines, each reel would take three to five seconds before landing the result. Hence, we also take some time, as specified in `spinDuration`, before showing the final random value. If you play the scene and click on the **Pull Lever** button, you should see the final result, as shown in the following screenshot:

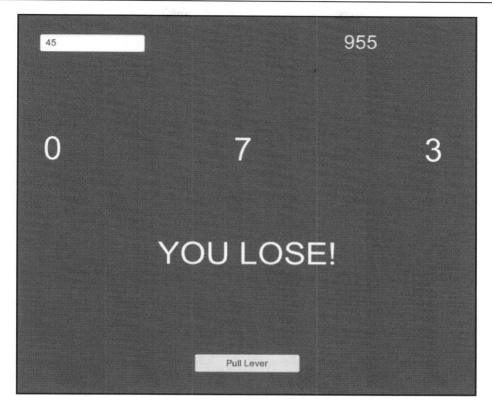

Our random slot game in action

Since your chance of winning is 1 out of 100, it quickly becomes boring as you lose several times consecutively. If you've ever played a slot machine, this is not how it works, or at least not anymore. Usually, you can have several wins during your play. Even though these small wins don't recoup your principal bet (and in the long run, most of the players go broke), the slot machines still occasionally render winning graphics and exciting sounds, which researchers referred to as losses disguised as wins.

So, instead of just one single way to win the jackpot, we'd like to modify the rules a bit so that it pays out smaller returns during the play session.

Weighted probability

Real slot machines have something called a **Paytable and Reel Strips (PARS)** sheet, which is like the complete design document of the machine. The PARS sheet is used to specify what the payout percentage is, the winning patterns, what their prizes are, and so on. Obviously, the number of the payout prizes and the frequencies of such wins need to be carefully selected so that the house (the slot machine) always wins in the long run, while making sure to return something to the players from time to time to make the machine attractive to play. This is known as payback percentage or **Return To Player (RTP)**. For example, a slot machine with a 90 percent RTP means that, over time, the machine will return an average of 90 percent of all bets to the players.

In this demo, we'll not be focusing on choosing the optimal value for the house to yield specific wins over time, nor maintaining a particular payback percentage. Rather, we'll be demonstrating weighting probability to specific symbols, so that they show up more times than usual. So, let's say we'd like to make the zero symbol to appear 20 percent more than usual on the first and third reel, and return half of the bet as a payout. In other words, a player will only lose half of their bet if they got zero symbols on the first and third reels, essentially disguising a loss as a small win. Currently, the zero symbol has a probability of 1/10th (0.1), or 10 percent probability, of occurring. We'll change this now to a 30 percent chance of zero landing on the first and third reels, as shown in the following `SlotMachineWeighted.cs` file (remember to switch to the `SlotMachineWeighted` component in the example code!):

```
using UnityEngine;
using System.Collections;
using UnityEngine.UI;

public class SlotMachineWeighted : MonoBehaviour {
  public float spinDuration = 2.0f;
  public int numberOfSym = 10;

  public Text firstReel;
  public Text secondReel;
  public Text thirdReel;
  public Text betResult;

  public Text totalCredits;
  public InputField inputBet;

  private bool startSpin = false;
  private bool firstReelSpinned = false;
  private bool secondReelSpinned = false;
```

```
private bool thirdReelSpinned = false;
private int betAmount = 100;
private int credits = 1000;

private ArrayList weightedReelPoll = new ArrayList();
private int zeroProbability = 30;
private int firstReelResult = 0;
private int secondReelResult = 0;
private int thirdReelResult = 0;
private float elapsedTime = 0.0f;
```

New variable declarations are added, such as zeroProbability to specify the probability percentage of the zero symbols to land on the first and third reels. The weightedReelPoll array list will be used to fill all the symbols (zero to nine) according to their distribution, so that we can later pick one randomly from the poll, as we did in our earlier FSM example. Then we initialize the list in our Start() method, as shown in the following code:

```
void Start () {
  for (int i = 0; i < zeroProbability; i++) {
    weightedReelPoll.Add(0);
  }
  int remainingValuesProb = (100 - zeroProbability)/9;
  for (int j = 1; j < 10; j++) {
    for (int k = 0; k < remainingValuesProb; k++) {
      weightedReelPoll.Add(j);
    }
  }
}
```

And the following is our revised checkBet() method. Instead of just one jackpot win option, we are now considering five conditions of *jackpot, loss disguised as a win, near miss, any two symbols matched on the first and third row*, and of course the *lose* condition:

```
void checkBet() {
  if (firstReelResult == secondReelResult && secondReelResult ==
thirdReelResult) {
    betResult.text = "JACKPOT!";
    credits += betAmount * 50;
  }
  else if (firstReelResult == 0 && thirdReelResult == 0) {
    betResult.text = "YOU WIN " + (betAmount/2).ToString();
    credits -= (betAmount/2);
  }
  else if (firstReelResult == secondReelResult) {
    betResult.text = "AWW... ALMOST JACKPOT!";
  }
```

```
    else if (firstReelResult == thirdReelResult) {
      betResult.text = "YOU WIN " + (betAmount*2).ToString();
      credits -= (betAmount*2);
    }
    else {
      betResult.text = "YOU LOSE!";
      credits -= betAmount;
    }
  }
```

In the `checkBet()` method, we designed our slot machine to return 50 times the bet if they hit the jackpot; to lose 50 percent of their bet if the first and third reels are zero; and to win two times if the first and third reels are matched with any other symbol. As in the previous example, we generate values for the three reels in the `FixedUpdate()` method, as shown in the following code:

```
    void FixedUpdate () {
      if (startSpin) {
        elapsedTime += Time.deltaTime;
        int randomSpinResult = Random.Range(0, numberOfSym);
        if (!firstReelSpinned) {
          firstReel.text = randomSpinResult.ToString();
          if (elapsedTime >= spinDuration) {
            int weightedRandom = Random.Range(0, weightedReelPoll.Count);
                    firstReel.text =
weightedReelPoll[weightedRandom].ToString();
            firstReelResult = (int)weightedReelPoll[weightedRandom];
            firstReelSpinned = true;
            elapsedTime = 0;
          }
        }
        else if (!secondReelSpinned) {
          secondReel.text = randomSpinResult.ToString();
          if (elapsedTime >= spinDuration) {
            secondReelResult = randomSpinResult;
            secondReelSpinned = true;
            elapsedTime = 0;
          }
        }
    ...
```

For the first reel, during the spinning period, we show the real random values as they occur. But once the time is up, we choose the value from our poll that is already populated with symbols according to the probability distributions. So, our zero symbols would have 30 percent more chance of occurring than the rest, as shown in the following screenshot:

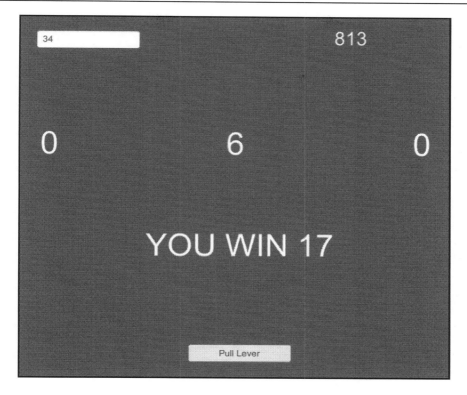

A loss disguised as a win

In reality, the player is losing on his bets if you get two zero symbols on the first and third reel; however, we make it seem like a win. It's just a lame message here, but if we can combine it with nice graphics, maybe with fireworks and a nice winning sound effects, this can really work.

Near miss

If the first and second reels return the same symbol, then we have to provide the near miss effect to the players by returning the random value to the third reel close to the second one. We can do this by checking the third random spin result first. If the random value is the same as the first and second results, then this is a jackpot, and we shouldn't alter the result.

But if it's not, then we should modify the result so that it is close enough to the other two. Check the comments in the following code:

```
else if (!thirdReelSpinned) {
        thirdReel.text = randomSpinResult.ToString();
        if (elapsedTime >= spinDuration) {
          if ((firstReelResult == secondReelResult) &&
            randomSpinResult != firstReelResult) {
            //the first two reels have resulted the same symbol
            //but unfortunately the third reel missed
            //so instead of giving a random number we'll return a symbol
which is one less than the other 2
            randomSpinResult = firstReelResult - 1;
            if (randomSpinResult < firstReelResult) randomSpinResult =
firstReelResult - 1;
            if (randomSpinResult > firstReelResult) randomSpinResult =
firstReelResult + 1;
            if (randomSpinResult < 0) randomSpinResult = 0;
            if (randomSpinResult > 9) randomSpinResult = 9;

                        thirdReel.text = randomSpinResult.ToString();
            thirdReelResult = randomSpinResult;
          }
          else {
            int weightedRandom = Random.Range(0, weightedReelPoll.Count);
                        thirdReel.text =
weightedReelPoll[weightedRandom].ToString();
            thirdReelResult = (int)weightedReelPoll[weightedRandom];
          }
          startSpin = false;
          elapsedTime = 0;
          firstReelSpinned = false;
          secondReelSpinned = false;
          checkBet();
        }
      }
    }
  }
```

And if that *near miss* happens, you should see it as shown in the following screenshot:

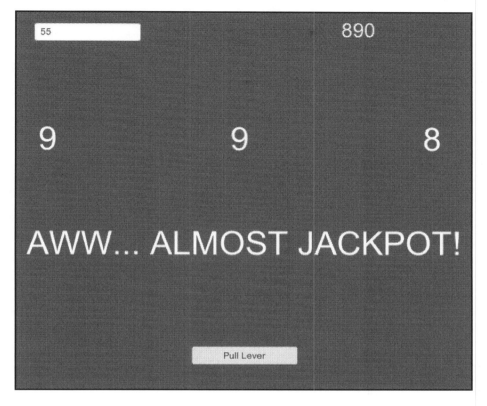

A near miss

We can go even further by adjusting the probability in real time, based on the bet amount (but that'd be too creepy). Finally, we could add a *Game Over* message that appears when the player has bet all their money.

Summary

In this chapter, we learned about the applications of probability in-game AI design. We experimented with some of the techniques by implementing them in Unity3D. As a bonus, we also learned about the basics of how a slot machine works, and implemented a simple slot machine game using Unity3D. Probability in game AI is about making the game and the characters seem more realistic by adding uncertainty to their behavior, so that the players cannot predict the outcome.

In the next chapter, we will take a look at implementing sensors, and how they can be used to make our AI aware of its surroundings.

Further reading

To further study the advanced techniques on probability in game AI, such as decision making under uncertainty using Bayesian techniques, I recommend reading *AI for Game Developers* by David M. Bourg and Glenn Seeman.

4
Implementing Sensors

As we discussed earlier, a character AI system needs to be aware of its surrounding environment: for example, NPCs need to know where the obstacles are, where the player is looking, if they are in the player's sight, and a lot more. The quality of the artificial intelligence of our NPCs depends, for the most part, on the information they can get from the environment. Based on that information, the AI-powered characters can decide on which action to execute. If there's not enough information, characters might show unusual behaviors, such as choosing the wrong places to take cover, idling, or looping in strange actions without knowing how to proceed. A quick search for *AI glitches* on YouTube opens the door to a huge collection of funny behaviors of AIs that are common, even in AAA games.

Theoretically, it is possible give to the NPCs all of the information they need directly from the computer's memory: after all, NPCs live in memory, and share every bit of information with the game. However, using a proper design pattern allow us to obtain two significant properties: firstly, the code will be more readable, modular, and maintainable; secondly, if characters can access only the information they need and that they can physically obtain, then the code will be more efficient and their behavior realistic.

In this chapter, we will look at the following topics:

- We will introduce such a design pattern: the sensory systems
- We will discover what a sensory system is, and how to implement two senses—sight and touch—in Unity
- We will build a demo where we can see our sensory system in action

Basic sensory systems

An AI sensory system emulates senses such as sight, hearing, and even smell to get information from other game objects. In such a system, the NPCs need to examine the environment and check for such senses periodically based on their particular interest.

In a minimal sensory system, we have two principal elements: `Aspect` and `Sense`. Every sense is capable of perceiving a specific aspect: for instance, an NPC with the sense of hearing can perceive the *sound* (the aspect) emitted by another game object, or a zombie NPC can use its smell sense to prey on the player's brain. As in real life, NPCs are not forced to use a single sense; they can have many such as sight, smell, and touch.

For our demo, we are going to implement a base interface, called Sense, that we'll use to implement custom senses. In this chapter, we'll implement sight and touch senses. Sight is what animals use to see the world around them; if our AI character sees an enemy, we receive an event in our code so that we can take some action. Likewise, with touch, when an enemy gets too close, we want to be able to sense that. Finally, we'll implement a minimal `Aspect` class that our senses can perceive.

Scene setup

Let's get started by setting up our scene:

1. Let's create a few walls to block the line-of-sight from our AI character to the enemy. We make these out of short—but wide—cubes that have been grouped under an empty game object called **Obstacles**.
2. We add a plane as a floor.
3. Finally, we add a directional light so that we can see what is going on in our scene.

We represent the player with a tank, similar to what we used in our first example, and we represent the NPCs with simple cubes. We also have a **Target** object to show us where the tank is moving in our scene. Our scene hierarchy should look similar to the following screenshot:

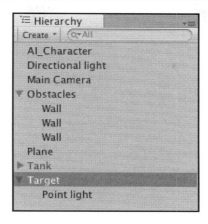

How our hierarchy is set up

Now, let's position the tank, AI character, and walls randomly around in our scene. Make sure to increase the size of the plane to something that looks good. Fortunately, in this demo, all the objects are locked on the plane, and there is no simulated gravity so that nothing can fall off the plane. Also, be sure to adjust the camera so that we can have a clear view of the following scene:

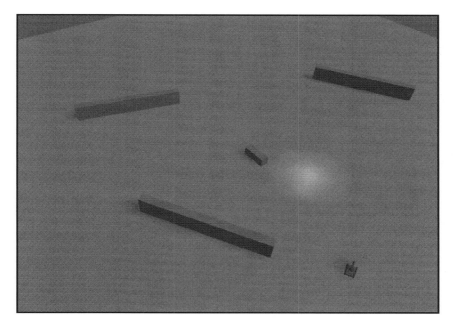

The space that our tank and player will wander in

Now that we have the basics set up, let's look at how to implement the tank, AI character, and aspects for our player character.

The player's tank and the aspect class

The Target object is a simple sphere object with the mesh render disabled. We have also created a point light and made it a child of our Target object. Make sure that the light is centered, or it will not be very helpful.

Look at the following code in the Target.cs file:

```
using UnityEngine;

public class Target : MonoBehaviour {

    void Update ()
    {
        int button = 0;

        //Get the point of the hit position when the mouse is being clicked
        if(Input.GetMouseButtonDown(button))
        {
            Ray ray = Camera.main.ScreenPointToRay(Input.mousePosition);
            RaycastHit hitInfo;
            if (Physics.Raycast(ray.origin, ray.direction, out hitInfo))
            {
                Vector3 targetPosition = hitInfo.point;
                transform.position = targetPosition;
            }
        }
    }
}
```

Attach this script to the Target object. The script detects the mouse-click event, and then, using the raycasting technique, detects the mouse-click location on the plane in the 3D space, and updates the Target object's position in our scene.

The player's tank

The player's tank is the simple tank model we used in the previous chapter, with a non-kinematic rigid body component attached. We need the rigid body component to generate trigger events whenever we do collision detection with AI characters and environment objects. Finally, we need to assign the `Player` tag to our tank.

As we can easily see from its name, the `PlayerTank` script controls the player's tank. The following is the code for the `PlayerTank.cs` file:

```
using UnityEngine;

public class PlayerTank : MonoBehaviour {
  public Transform targetTransform;
  public float movementSpeed, rotSpeed;

  void Update () {
    //Stop once you reached near the target position
    if (Vector3.Distance(transform.position,
      targetTransform.position) < 5.0f)
      return;

    //Calculate direction vector from current position to target
//position
    Vector3 tarPos = targetTransform.position;
    tarPos.y = transform.position.y;
    Vector3 dirRot = tarPos - transform.position;

    //Build a Quaternion for this new rotation vector
    //using LookRotation method
    Quaternion tarRot = Quaternion.LookRotation(dirRot);

    //Move and rotate with interpolation
    transform.rotation= Quaternion.Slerp(transform.rotation,
        tarRot, rotSpeed * Time.deltaTime);

    transform.Translate(new Vector3(0, 0,
        movementSpeed * Time.deltaTime));
  }
}
```

This script retrieves the `Target` position on the map and updates the tank's destination point and direction accordingly:

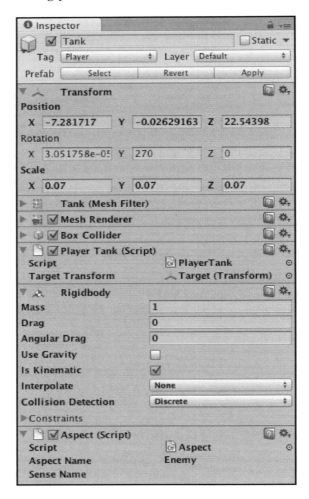

The properties of our Tank object

After we assign the preceding script to the tank, be sure to assign the `Target` object to the `targetTransform` variable.

Aspect

Next, let's take a look at the `Aspect.cs` class. `Aspect` is a very simple class with just one public property, called `aspectName`. That's all the variables we need in this chapter. Whenever our AI character senses something, we'll check this against the `aspectName` to see if it's the aspect that the AI has been looking for.

The code in the `Aspect.cs` file is as follows:

```
using UnityEngine;

public class Aspect : MonoBehaviour {
  public enum aspect {
    Player,
    Enemy
  }
  public aspect aspectName;
}
```

Attach this aspect script to our player tank and set the `aspectName` property as `Enemy`:

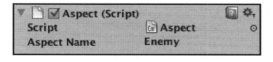

Setting the aspect to look out for

AI characters

In this example, the AI characters roam around the scene in a random direction. They have two senses: `Sight` and `Touch`. The `Sight` sense checks whether the enemy aspect is within a set visible range and distance. The `Touch` sense, instead, detects if the enemy aspect has collided with the box collider around the character. As we have seen previously, our player tank has the `Enemy` aspect. Consequently, these senses are triggered when they detect the player tank.

For now, let's look at the script we use to move the NPCs around. The following is the code in the `Wander.cs` file:

```csharp
using UnityEngine;
using System.Collections;

public class Wander : MonoBehaviour {
  private Vector3 tarPos;

  private float movementSpeed = 5.0f;
  private float rotSpeed = 2.0f;
  private float minX, maxX, minZ, maxZ;

  // Use this for initialization
  void Start () {
    minX = -45.0f;
    maxX = 45.0f;

    minZ = -45.0f;
    maxZ = 45.0f;

    //Get Wander Position
    GetNextPosition();
  }
  // Update is called once per frame
  void Update () {
    // Check if we're near the destination position
    if (Vector3.Distance(tarPos, transform.position) <= 5.0f)
      GetNextPosition(); //generate new random position

    // Set up quaternion for rotation toward destination
    Quaternion tarRot = Quaternion.LookRotation(tarPos -
        transform.position);

    // Update rotation and translation
    transform.rotation = Quaternion.Slerp(transform.rotation, tarRot,
        rotSpeed * Time.deltaTime);

    transform.Translate(new Vector3(0, 0,
        movementSpeed * Time.deltaTime));
  }

  void GetNextPosition() {
    tarPos = new Vector3(Random.Range(minX, maxX), 0.5f,
        Random.Range(minZ, maxZ));
  }
}
```

The Wander script generates a new random position in a specified range whenever an AI character reaches its current destination point. Then, the Update method rotates the NPCs and moves them toward their new destination. Attach this script to our AI character so that it can move around in the scene.

Sense

The Sense class is the interface of our sensory system that the other custom senses can implement. It defines two virtual methods, Initialize and UpdateSense, which are executed from the Start and Update methods, respectively, and which we can override when implementing custom senses.

Here, we are showing the code that's in the Sense.cs file:

```
using UnityEngine;

public class Sense : MonoBehaviour {
  public bool bDebug = true;
  public Aspect.aspect aspectName = Aspect.aspect.Enemy;
  public float detectionRate = 1.0f;

  protected float elapsedTime = 0.0f;

  protected virtual void Initialize() { }
  protected virtual void UpdateSense() { }

  // Use this for initialization
  void Start () {
    elapsedTime = 0.0f;
    Initialize();
  }
  // Update is called once per frame
  void Update () {
    UpdateSense();
  }
}
```

The basic properties of this script are the intervals between two consecutive sensing operations and the name of the aspect it should look for. This script is not attached to any of our objects; instead, it is used as a base for specific senses, such as `Sight` and `Touch`.

Sight

The sight sense detects whether a specific aspect is within the perception field of the character. If it perceives anything, it takes the specified action.

The code in the `Sight.cs` file is as follows:

```
using UnityEngine;

public class Sight: Sense {
  public int FieldOfView = 45;
  public int ViewDistance = 100;

  private Transform playerTrans;
  private Vector3 rayDirection;

  protected override void Initialize() {

    //Find player position
    playerTrans =
GameObject.FindGameObjectWithTag("Player").transform;
  }

  // Update is called once per frame
  protected override void UpdateSense() {
    elapsedTime += Time.deltaTime;

    // Detect perspective sense if within the detection rate
    if (elapsedTime >= detectionRate) DetectAspect();
  }

  //Detect perspective field of view for the AI Character
  void DetectAspect() {
    RaycastHit hit;

    //Direction from current position to player position
    rayDirection = playerTrans.position -
        transform.position;

    //Check the angle between the AI character's forward
    //vector and the direction vector between player and AI
    if ((Vector3.Angle(rayDirection, transform.forward)) < FieldOfView) {
```

```
    // Detect if player is within the field of view
    if (Physics.Raycast(transform.position, rayDirection,
        out hit, ViewDistance)) {
      Aspect aspect =
      hit.collider.GetComponent<Aspect>();

      if (aspect != null) {
        //Check the aspect
        if (aspect.aspectName == aspectName) {
          print("Enemy Detected");
        }
      }
    }
  }
 }
}
```

We need to implement the `Initialize` and `UpdateSense` methods that are called from the `Start` and `Update` methods of the parent `Sense` class, respectively. Then, in the `DetectAspect` method, we first check the angle between the player and the AI's current direction. If it's in the field of view range, we shoot a ray in the direction where the player tank is located. The length of the ray is the value in the visible distance property. The `Raycast` method returns when it first hits another object. Then, we check this against the aspect component and the aspect name. In this way, even if the player is in the visible range, the AI character will not be able to see the player if they're hidden behind a wall.

The `OnDrawGizmos` method draws lines based on the perspective field, described by the view angle and viewing distance, so that we can see the AI character's line-of-sight in the editor window during playtesting. Attach this script to our AI character, and be sure that the aspect name is set to `Enemy`.

This method can be illustrated as follows:

```
void OnDrawGizmos() {
  if (!Application.isEditor|| playerTrans == null) return;

  Debug.DrawLine(transform.position, playerTrans.position, Color.red);

  Vector3 frontRayPoint = transform.position +
      (transform.forward * ViewDistance);

  //Approximate perspective visualization
  Vector3 leftRayPoint = Quaternion.Euler(0,FieldOfView * 0.5f ,0) *
frontRayPoint;
  Vector3 rightRayPoint = Quaternion.Euler(0, - FieldOfView*0.5f, 0) *
frontRayPoint;
```

```
        Debug.DrawLine(transform.position, frontRayPoint, Color.green);

        Debug.DrawLine(transform.position, leftRayPoint, Color.green);

        Debug.DrawLine(transform.position, rightRayPoint, Color.green);
    }
}
```

Touch

Another sense we're going to implement is Touch.cs, which is triggered when the player entity is within a specific range of the AI entity. Our AI character has a box collider component, and its **Is Trigger** flag is on.

The code in the Touch.cs file is as follows:

```
using UnityEngine;

public class Touch : Sense {
    void OnTriggerEnter(Collider other) {
        Aspect aspect = other.GetComponent<Aspect>();
        if (aspect != null) {
            //Check the aspect
            if (aspect.aspectName == aspectName) {
                print("Enemy Touch Detected");
            }
        }
    }
}
```

We need to implement the OnTriggerEnter event that is fired whenever the collider component collides with another collider component. Since our tank entity also has a collider and rigid body components, a collision event occurs as soon as the colliders of the AI character and player tank coincide. The following screenshot shows the box collider of our enemy AI that we are using to implement the Touch sense:

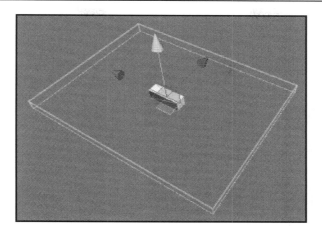

The collider component around our player

In the following screenshot, we can see how our AI character is set up:

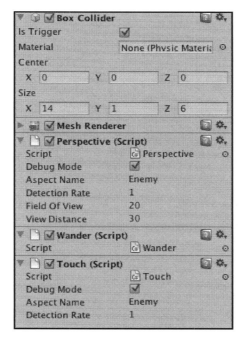

Properties of our player

Inside the `OnTriggerEnter` method, we access the aspect component of the other collider entity and check if the name of the aspect is the same aspect that this AI character is looking for. For demonstration purposes, we will print out in the console that the character detects the enemy aspect by touch sense. In a real game, we would not print the event, but rather trigger other actions, such as turning to face an enemy and then chasing, attacking, and so on.

Testing

Now, play the game in Unity3D and move the player tank near the wandering AI character by clicking on the ground. You should see the message **Enemy touch detected** in the console log window whenever our AI character gets close to our player tank:

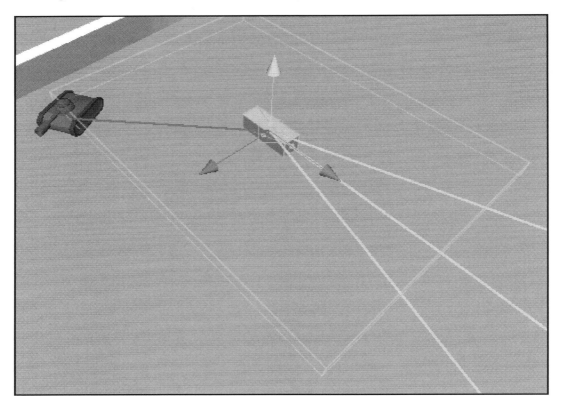

Our player and tank in action

The previous screenshot shows an AI agent with touch and perspective senses looking for an enemy aspect. Move the player tank in front of the AI character, and you'll get the **Enemy detected** message. If you go into the editor view while running the game, you should see the debug drawings being rendered. This is because of the `OnDrawGizmos` method, implemented in the `Sight` sense class.

Summary

This chapter introduces the concept of using sensors in implementing game AI, and we implemented two senses, `Sight` and `Touch`, for our AI character. The sensory system is just the first element of the decision-making system of a whole AI system. For instance, we can use the sensory system in combination with a behavior system to execute certain behaviors for certain senses, or we can use an FSM to change from the patrol state to chase and attack states once we have detected that there's an enemy within the AI's line of sight.

We will cover how to apply behavior tree systems in `Chapter 9`, *Behavior Trees*. In the meantime, in the next chapter, we'll look at how to implement flocking behaviors in Unity3D, as well as how to implement Craig Reynold's flocking algorithm.

5

Flocking

In the early summer evenings, you have probably seen flocks of birds flying in the sky. You have probably noted how they seem to move as a single living object: they all move in a particular direction, turn around, and grow and shrink. In games, a flocking system aims to replicate this behavior: we want to implement an algorithm to move many objects as an organic group.

In games, we call each element of a flock a **boid**. To implement a flocking behavior, we do not need to tell each boid what to do; instead, all we need to do is implement a few rules for each boid to follow so that they can flock on their own. In fact, flocking is an excellent example of emergent behavior: each boid reacts exclusively to its neighbor's behaviors; nevertheless, the flock seems to move as if someone were coordinating it.

In this chapter, we will learn what these rules are and how to implement them in Unity3D. We will implement two variations of flocking in this chapter. The first one is based on an old flocking behavior demo that has been circulating in the Unity community since Unity 2.0. The second variation is based on Craig Reynold's original flocking algorithm from 1986.

In this chapter we will cover the following topics:

- An overview of the basic flocking behavior and how to implement it
- An alternative implementation of the flocking behavior

Basic flocking behavior

As we said in the introduction to this chapter, we can describe a flocking behavior by using just three intuitive rules:

- **Separation**: Also called **short-range repulsion**, this instructs each boid to maintain a minimum distance with neighboring boids to avoid collisions. You can imagine this rule as a force that pushes the boid away from the others.

- **Alignment**: According to this rule, each boid tends to move in the same direction as the flock (measured as the average direction of all the individual boids).
- **Cohesion**: Also called **long-range attraction**, this instructs each boid to move toward the center of mass of the flock (measured by averaging the position of each boid in the flock). You can imagine this rule as a force that pushes the boid toward the center of the flock.

In this section, we'll create our scene with flocks of objects, and will implement the flocking behavior in C#. For this first version, we'll compute all the rules by ourselves. Also, we'll create a *boid commander* that will lead the crowd so that we can control the general position of the flock.

You can see the **Hierarchy** scene in the following screenshot. As you can see, we have several boid entities, named **UnityFlock**, under a controller named **UnityFlockController**. **UnityFlock** entities are individual boid objects that refer to their parent **UnityFlockController** entity, using it as a leader. The controller updates the next destination point randomly once it reaches the current destination point:

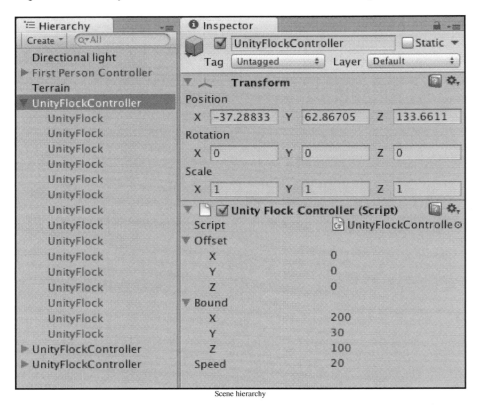

Scene hierarchy

UnityFlock is a prefab with just a cube mesh and a **UnityFlock** script. We can use any other mesh representation for this prefab to represent something more interesting, such as birds.

Individual behavior

Boid is a term that was coined by Craig Reynold that refers to some bird-like object. We use this term to describe each individual object in our flock. Now, let's implement our boid behavior. You can find the behavior that controls each boid in our flock in the UnityFlock.cs script, which we'll examine now:

1. The code in the UnityFlock.cs file is as follows:

```
using UnityEngine;
using System.Collections;

public class UnityFlock : MonoBehaviour {
   public float minSpeed = 20.0f;
   public float turnSpeed = 20.0f;
   public float randomFreq = 20.0f;
   public float randomForce = 20.0f;

   //alignment variables
   public float toOriginForce = 50.0f;
   public float toOriginRange = 100.0f;

   public float gravity = 2.0f;

   //seperation variables
   public float avoidanceRadius = 50.0f;
   public float avoidanceForce = 20.0f;

   //cohesion variables
   public float followVelocity = 4.0f;
   public float followRadius = 40.0f;

   //these variables control the movement of the boid
   private Transform origin;
   private Vector3 velocity;
   private Vector3 normalizedVelocity;
   private Vector3 randomPush;
   private Vector3 originPush;
   private Transform[] objects;
   private UnityFlock[] otherFlocks;
   private Transform transformComponent;
```

As public fields, we declare the input values for our algorithm. These can be set up and customized from the editor:

- We define the minimum movement speed (minSpeed) and rotation speed (turnSpeed) for our boid.
- randomFreq is used to determine how many times we want to update the randomPush value based on the randomForce value. This force is used to vary the velocity of the single boid and to make the flock movement look more realistic.
- toOriginRange specifies how much we want the flock to spread out. In other words, it represents the maximum distance from the flock's origin in which we want to maintain the boids (following the previously mentioned *cohesion* rule).
- The avoidanceRadius and avoidanceForce properties are used to maintain a minimum distance between individual boids (following the *separation* rule).
- followRadius and followVelocity are used to keep a minimum distance between the leader or origin of the flock. These are other elements that are used to comply with the cohesion rule of the flocking algorithm in this variation.
- origin will be the parent object that controls the whole group of flocking objects: in other words, the flock leader. Our boid needs to know about the other boids in the flock. Therefore, we use the objects and otherFlocks properties to store the neighboring boid's information.

2. This is the initialization method for our boid:

```
void Start () {
  randomFreq = 1.0f / randomFreq;

  //Assign the parent as origin
  origin = transform.parent;

  //Flock transform
  transformComponent = transform;

  //Temporary components
  Component[] tempFlocks= null;

  //Get all the unity flock components from the parent
  //transform in the group
  if (transform.parent) {
    tempFlocks = transform.parent.GetComponentsInChildren
        <UnityFlock>();
  }
```

```
//Assign and store all the flock objects in this group
objects = new Transform[tempFlocks.Length];
otherFlocks = new UnityFlock[tempFlocks.Length];

for (int i = 0;i<tempFlocks.Length;i++) {
  objects[i] = tempFlocks[i].transform;
  otherFlocks[i] = (UnityFlock)tempFlocks[i];
}

//Null Parent as the flock leader will be
//UnityFlockController object
transform.parent = null;

//Calculate random push depends on the random frequency
//provided
  StartCoroutine(UpdateRandom());
}
```

We set the parent of the object of our boid as `origin`, meaning that this will be the controller object for the other boids to follow. Then, we grab all the other boids in the group and store them in our own variables for later reference.

3. The `StartCoroutine` method starts the `UpdateRandom()` method as a coroutine:

```
IEnumerator UpdateRandom() {
  while (true) {
    randomPush = Random.insideUnitSphere * randomForce;
    yield return new WaitForSeconds(randomFreq +
        Random.Range(-randomFreq / 2.0f, randomFreq / 2.0f));
  }
}
```

4. The `UpdateRandom()` method updates the `randomPush` value throughout the game with an interval based on `randomFreq`. `Random.insideUnitSphere`, which returns a `Vector3` object with random *x*, *y*, and *z* values within a sphere with a radius of the `randomForce` value.

5. We wait for a certain random amount of time before resuming the `while(true)` loop to update the `randomPush` value again.

6. Now, here is our boid behavior's `Update()` method, which helps the boid entity comply with the three rules of the flocking algorithm:

```
void Update () {
  //Internal variables
  float speed = velocity.magnitude;
  Vector3 avgVelocity = Vector3.zero;
  Vector3 avgPosition = Vector3.zero;
  float count = 0;
  float f = 0.0f;
  float d = 0.0f;
  Vector3 myPosition = transformComponent.position;
  Vector3 forceV;
  Vector3 toAvg;
  Vector3 wantedVel;

  for (int i = 0;i<objects.Length;i++){
    Transform transform= objects[i];
    if (transform != transformComponent) {
      Vector3 otherPosition = transform.position;

      // Average position to calculate cohesion
      avgPosition += otherPosition;
      count++;

      //Directional vector from other flock to this flock
      forceV = myPosition - otherPosition;

      //Magnitude of that directional vector(Length)
      d= forceV.magnitude;

      //Add push value if the magnitude, the length of the
      //vector, is less than followRadius to the leader
      if (d < followRadius) {
        //calculate the velocity, the speed of the object, based
         //on the avoidance distance between flocks if the
        //current magnitude is less than the specified
        //avoidance radius
        if (d < avoidanceRadius) {
          f = 1.0f - (d / avoidanceRadius);
          if (d > 0) avgVelocity +=
              (forceV / d) * f * avoidanceForce;
        }
```

```
            //just keep the current distance with the leader
            f = d / followRadius;
            UnityFlock otherSealgull = otherFlocks[i];
            //we normalize the otherSealgull velocity vector to get
            //the direction of movement, then we set a new velocity
            avgVelocity += otherSealgull.normalizedVelocity * f *
                followVelocity;
        }
    }
}
```

The preceding code implements the separation rule. First, we check the distance between the current boid and the other boids, and then update the velocity accordingly, as explained in the comments in the preceding code block.

7. We now calculate the average velocity vector of the flock by dividing the current velocity vector with the number of boids in the flock:

```
if (count > 0) {
  //Calculate the average flock velocity(Alignment)
  avgVelocity /= count;

  //Calculate Center value of the flock(Cohesion)
  toAvg = (avgPosition / count) - myPosition;
}
else {
  toAvg = Vector3.zero;
}

//Directional Vector to the leader
forceV = origin.position -  myPosition;
d = forceV.magnitude;
f = d / toOriginRange;

//Calculate the velocity of the flock to the leader
if (d > 0) //if this void is not at the center of the flock
    originPush = (forceV / d) * f * toOriginForce;
```

```
        if (speed < minSpeed && speed > 0) {
          velocity = (velocity / speed) * minSpeed;
        }

        wantedVel = velocity;

        //Calculate final velocity
        wantedVel -= wantedVel *  Time.deltaTime;
        wantedVel += randomPush * Time.deltaTime;
        wantedVel += originPush * Time.deltaTime;
        wantedVel += avgVelocity * Time.deltaTime;
        wantedVel += toAvg.normalized * gravity * Time.deltaTime;

        //Final Velocity to rotate the flock into
        velocity = Vector3.RotateTowards(velocity, wantedVel,
            turnSpeed * Time.deltaTime, 100.00f);

        transformComponent.rotation =
    Quaternion.LookRotation(velocity);

        //Move the flock based on the calculated velocity
        transformComponent.Translate(velocity * Time.deltaTime,
            Space.World);

        //normalise the velocity
        normalizedVelocity = velocity.normalized;
      }
    }
```

8. We add up all the factors, such as `randomPush`, `originPush`, and `avgVelocity`, to calculate the final target velocity vector, `wantedVel`. We also update the current `velocity` to `wantedVel` with a linear interpolation by using the `Vector3.RotateTowards` method.

9. We move our boid based on the new velocity using the `Translate()` method.

10. As a final touch, we create a cube mesh, to which we add the **UnityFlock** script, and then save it as a prefab, as shown in the following screenshot:

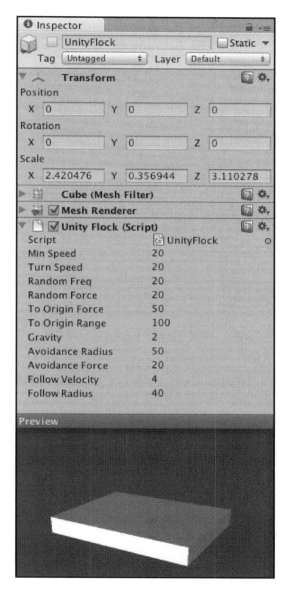

Unity flock prefab

Controller

Now, it is time to create the controller class. This class updates its own position so that the other individual boid objects know where to go. The `origin` variable in the preceding **UnityFlock** script contains a reference to this object.

The following is the code in the `UnityFlockController.cs` file:

```
using UnityEngine;
using System.Collections;

public class UnityFlockController : MonoBehaviour {
  public Vector3 offset;
  public Vector3 bound;
  public float speed = 100.0f;

  private Vector3 initialPosition;
  private Vector3 nextMovementPoint;

  // Use this for initialization
  void Start () {
    initialPosition = transform.position;
    CalculateNextMovementPoint();
  }

  // Update is called once per frame
  void Update () {
    transform.Translate(Vector3.forward * speed * Time.deltaTime);
    transform.rotation = Quaternion.Slerp(transform.rotation,
        Quaternion.LookRotation(nextMovementPoint -
        transform.position), 1.0f * Time.deltaTime);

    if (Vector3.Distance(nextMovementPoint,
        transform.position) <= 10.0f)
        CalculateNextMovementPoint();
  }
```

In the `Update()` method, we check whether our controller object is near the target destination point. If it is, we update the `nextMovementPoint` variable again with the `CalculateNextMovementPoint()` method we just discussed:

```
  void CalculateNextMovementPoint () {
    float posX = Random.Range(initialPosition.x - bound.x,
        initialPosition.x + bound.x);
    float posY = Random.Range(initialPosition.y - bound.y,
        initialPosition.y + bound.y);
    float posZ = Random.Range(initialPosition.z - bound.z,
```

```
        initialPosition.z + bound.z);

    nextMovementPoint = initialPosition + new Vector3(posX,
        posY, posZ);
    }
}
```

The `CalculateNextMovementPoint()` method finds the next random destination position in a range between the current position and the boundary vectors.

Finally, we put all of this together, as shown in the previous scene **Hierarchy** screenshot, which should give you flocks of squares flying around realistically in the sunset:

A demonstration of the flocking behavior using the Unity seagull sample

Alternative implementation

In this section, we will use the Unity physics engine to simplify the code a bit. In fact, in this example, we will attach a `rigidbody` component to our boids so that we can use `rigidbody` properties for the translation and steering behaviors of our boid. The `rigidbody` component is also useful to prevent our boids from overlapping with each other.

In this implementation, we have two components: the individual boid behavior and the controller behavior (the element that we referred to as the *flock controller* in the previous section). As before, the controller will be the object that the rest of the boids follow.

The code in the `Flock.cs` file is as follows:

```
using UnityEngine;
using System.Collections;
using System.Collections.Generic;

public class Flock : MonoBehaviour {
  internal FlockController controller;

  private new Rigidbody rigidbody;

  private void Start() {
      this.rigidbody = GetComponent<Rigidbody>();
  }

  void Update () {
    if (controller) {
      Vector3 relativePos = steer() * Time.deltaTime;

      if (relativePos != Vector3.zero)
          rigidbody.velocity = relativePos;

      // enforce minimum and maximum speeds for the boids
      float speed = rigidbody.velocity.magnitude;
      if (speed > controller.maxVelocity) {
        rigidbody.velocity = rigidbody.velocity.normalized *
          controller.maxVelocity;
      }
      else if (speed < controller.minVelocity) {
        rigidbody.velocity = rigidbody.velocity.normalized *
            controller.minVelocity;
      }
    }
  }
```

We will create a `FlockController` in a moment. In the meantime, in the `Update()` method in the previous code block, we will calculate the velocity of the boid using the `steer()` method and we will apply the result to the boid's `rigidbody` velocity. Next, we will check if the current speed of the `rigidbody` component is inside our controller's maximum and minimum velocity ranges. If not, we cap the velocity at the preset range:

```
private Vector3 steer () {
  Vector3 center = controller.flockCenter -
      transform.localPosition;  // cohesion

  Vector3 velocity = controller.flockVelocity -
      rigidbody.velocity;  // alignment

  Vector3 follow = controller.target.localPosition -
      transform.localPosition;  // follow leader

  Vector3 separation = Vector3.zero;

  foreach (Flock flock in controller.flockList) {
    if (flock != this) {
      Vector3 relativePos = transform.localPosition -
          flock.transform.localPosition;

      separation += relativePos / (relativePos.sqrMagnitude);
    }
  }

  // randomize
  Vector3 randomize = new Vector3( (Random.value * 2) - 1,
      (Random.value * 2) - 1, (Random.value * 2) - 1);

  randomize.Normalize();

  return (controller.centerWeight * center +
      controller.velocityWeight * velocity +
      controller.separationWeight * separation +
      controller.followWeight * follow +
      controller.randomizeWeight * randomize);
  }
}
```

The `steer()` method implements separation, cohesion, and alignment, and follows the leader rules of the flocking algorithm. Then, we sum up all the factors together with a random weight value. We use this **Flock (Script)**, together with the **Rigidbody** and **Sphere Collider** components, to create a **Flock** prefab, as shown in the following screenshot:

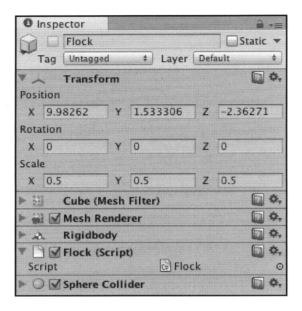

Flock

FlockController

This `FlockController` is similar to the one in the previous example. In addition to controlling the flock's speed and position, this script also instantiates the boids at runtime:

1. The code in the `FlockController.cs` file is as follows:

```
using UnityEngine;
using System.Collections;
using System.Collections.Generic;

public class FlockController : MonoBehaviour {
    public float minVelocity = 1;   //Min Velocity
    public float maxVelocity = 8;   //Max Flock speed
    public int flockSize = 20;   //Number of flocks in the group

    //How far the boids should stick to the center (the more
```

```
//weight stick closer to the center)
public float centerWeight = 1;

public float velocityWeight = 1;   //Alignment behavior

//How far each boid should be separated within the flock
public float separationWeight = 1;

//How close each boid should follow to the leader (the more
//weight make the closer follow)
public float followWeight = 1;

//Additional Random Noise
public float randomizeWeight = 1;

public Flock prefab;
public Transform target;

//Center position of the flock in the group
internal Vector3 flockCenter;
internal Vector3 flockVelocity;   //Average Velocity

public ArrayList flockList = new ArrayList();

void Start () {
  for (int i = 0; i < flockSize; i++) {
    Flock flock = Instantiate(prefab, transform.position,
        transform.rotation) as Flock;
    flock.transform.parent = transform;
    flock.controller = this;
    flockList.Add(flock);
  }
}
```

2. We declare all the `public` properties to implement the flocking algorithm and then start with the generation of the boid objects based on the flock size input.

3. We set up the controller class and the parent `Transform` object like we did last time.

4. We add every boid object we create to the `flockList` array. The `target` variable accepts an entity to be used as a moving leader. In this example, we create a sphere entity as a moving target leader for our flock:

```
void Update () {
  //Calculate the Center and Velocity of the whole flock group
  Vector3 center = Vector3.zero;
  Vector3 velocity = Vector3.zero;
```

```
foreach (Flock flock in flockList) {
  center += flock.transform.localPosition;
  velocity += flock.rigidbody.velocity;
}

flockCenter = center / flockSize;
flockVelocity = velocity / flockSize;
  }
}
```

5. In the `Update()` method, we keep updating the average center and velocity of the flock. These are the values that are referenced from our boid object, and are used to adjust the cohesion and alignment properties with the controller:

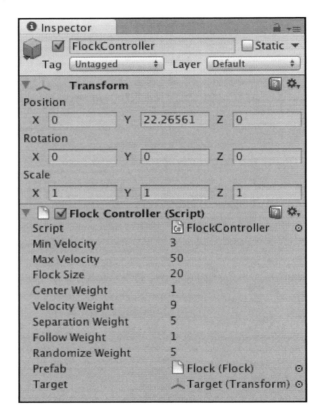

Flock controller

6. We need to implement our **Target** entity with the **Target Movement (Script)**. The movement script is the same as what we saw in our previous Unity3D sample controller's movement script:

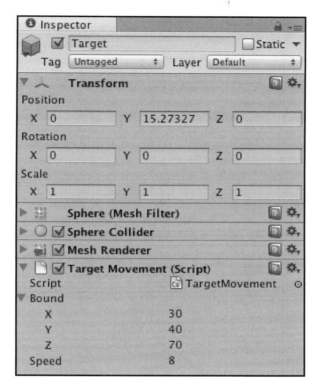

Target entity with the TargetMovement script

7. Here is how our `TargetMovement` script works: we pick a random point nearby for the target to move to, and when we get close to that point, we pick a new one.

The code in the `TargetMovement.cs` file is as follows:

```
using UnityEngine;
using System.Collections;

public class TargetMovement : MonoBehaviour {
  //Move target around circle with tangential speed
  public Vector3 bound;
  public float speed = 100.0f;

  private Vector3 initialPosition;
```

```
private Vector3 nextMovementPoint;

void Start () {
  initialPosition = transform.position;
  CalculateNextMovementPoint();
}
void CalculateNextMovementPoint () {
  float posX = Random.Range(initialPosition.x = bound.x,
      initialPosition.x+bound.x);
  float posY = Random.Range(initialPosition.y = bound.y,
      initialPosition.y+bound.y);
  float posZ = Random.Range(initialPosition.z = bound.z,
      initialPosition.z+bound.z);

  nextMovementPoint = initialPosition+
      new Vector3(posX, posY, posZ);
}
void Update () {
  transform.Translate(Vector3.forward * speed * Time.deltaTime);
  transform.rotation = Quaternion.Slerp(transform.rotation,
      Quaternion.LookRotation(nextMovementPoint -
      transform.position), 1.0f * Time.deltaTime);

  if (Vector3.Distance(nextMovementPoint, transform.position)
      <= 10.0f) CalculateNextMovementPoint();
}
}
```

8. After we put everything together, we should have nice flocking cube boids flying around in our scene, chasing that target:

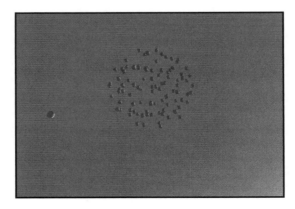

Flocking with Craig Reynold's algorithm

Summary

In this chapter, we learned how to implement flocking behaviors in two ways. First, we examined and learned how to implement a basic flocking algorithm using nothing other than our scripts. Next, we implemented the same algorithm using Unity's **Rigidbody** component to control the boid's movement and **Sphere Collider** to avoid collision with other boids.

In our example, we always referred to boids as bird-like entities. However, we can use flocking for a lot of other applications: fishes swimming in the sea, sheep grazing on a plane, a swarm of insects, and even groups of people walking on the street can show a flocking behavior. To adapt the algorithm to different scenarios, we just need to change the values of the flocking rules, and eventually, lock the movement to a plane.

In the next chapter, we, go beyond random movement and take a look at how to follow a specific path. This is the first step toward learning how to avoid obstacles that are in your way.

6

Path-Following and Steering Behaviors

This is a short chapter in which we will implement two Unity3D scenes to explore steering behaviors. In the first example, we will set up a scene with a path and implement a script to make an entity follow this path. In the second example, we will set up a scene with a couple of obstacles, and program an entity to reach a target while avoiding the obstacles.

Obstacle avoidance is a fundamental behavior for game characters when moving around and interacting with the game world. However, usually, obstacle avoidance is used in conjunction with other navigation systems (such as pathfinding or crowd simulations). In this chapter, we will use the systems to make sure that we avoid the other agents and reach the target. We will not talk about how fast the character will reach a destination, and we will not calculate the shortest path to the target, as we'll talk about these in the next chapter.

In this chapter, we'll look at the basics of movement, such as the following:

- Following a path
- Avoiding obstacles

Following a path

A **path** is a sequence of points in the game, connecting a point, A, to another point, B. There are many ways to build a path. Usually, a path is automatically generated by other game systems, such as pathfinding (see the next chapter); however, in our example, we, use a very basic system: we will construct the path by hand by using **waypoints**. We will write a script called `Path.cs` and store all the waypoint positions in a `Vector3` array. Then, from the editor, we will enter those positions manually. It's a bit of a tedious process right now, but we don't want to make things too complicated. Fortunately, since the number of waypoints that we are creating here is not that substantial, the operation should not take too much time:

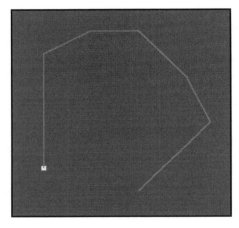

Object path

First, we create an empty game entity and add our path script component, as shown in the following screenshot:

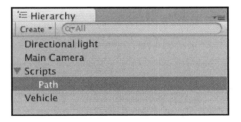

Here is how the Hierarchy is organized

Then, we populate our **Point A** variable with all the points we want to include in our path:

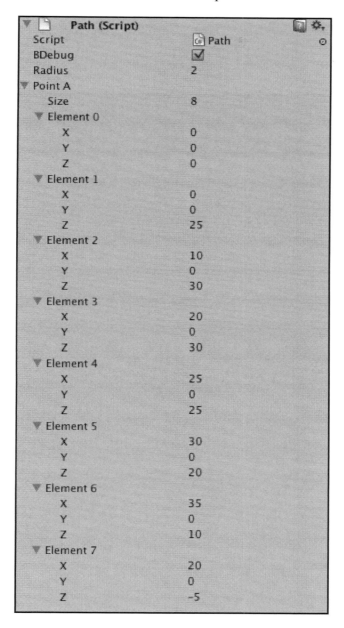

Properties of our path script

The previous list shows the waypoints needed to create the path that was described earlier. The other two properties are debug mode and radius. If the debug mode property is checked, the path formed by the positions entered will be drawn as gizmos in the editor window. The radius property is a range value for the path-following entities to use so that they know when they've reached a particular waypoint if they are close enough, where *enough* is the radius value. In fact, reaching the exact position of a waypoint is almost impossible, due to floating point approximation; this range radius value provides an effective way for the path-following agents to understand if they are near enough.

Path script

Let's take a look at the path script itself, which is responsible for managing the path for our objects. Consider the following code in the Path.cs file:

```
using UnityEngine;
using System.Collections;

public class Path : MonoBehaviour {
  public bool bDebug = true;
  public float Radius = 2.0f;
  public Vector3[] pointA;

  public float Length {
    get {
      return pointA.Length;
    }
  }

  public Vector3 GetPoint(int index) {
    return pointA[index];
  }

  void OnDrawGizmos() {
    if (!bDebug) return;

    for (int i = 0; i <pointA.Length; i++) {
      if (i + 1<pointA.Length) {
        Debug.DrawLine(pointA[i], pointA[i + 1],
          Color.red);
      }
    }
  }
}
```

As you can see, that is a straightforward script. It has a `Length` property that returns the length and size of the waypoint array, if requested. The `GetPoint` method returns the `Vector3` position of a particular waypoint at a specified index in the array. Then, we have the `OnDrawGizmos` method, which is called by the Unity3D frame to draw components in the editor environment. The drawing here won't be rendered in the game view unless the gizmos flag, located in the top right corner of the game view, is turned on.

Path-following agents

As a next step, we need to create the character that will follow the path; in our example, this *agent* is just a cube object. Readers can replace the cube later with whatever 3D models they want. After we create the script, we add the **VehicleFollowing** script component to it, as shown in the following screenshot:

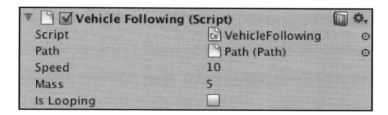

The properties of our VehicleFollowing script

The script takes a couple of parameters: first is the reference to the path object it needs to follow; then, we have the **Speed** and **Mass** properties, which we need in order to calculate the character's acceleration. The **Is Looping** flag, if checked, makes this entity follow the path continuously in a closed loop. Let's take a look at the following code in the `VehicleFollowing.cs` file:

```
using UnityEngine;
using System.Collections;

public class VehicleFollowing : MonoBehaviour {
    public Path path;
    public float speed = 20.0f;
    public float mass = 5.0f;
    public bool isLooping = true;

    //Actual speed of the vehicle
    private float curSpeed;
```

```
private int curPathIndex;
private float pathLength;
private Vector3 targetPoint;

Vector3 velocity;
```

First, we initialize the properties and set up the direction of our velocity vector with the entity's forward vector in the `Start` method, as shown in the following code:

```
void Start () {
  pathLength = path.Length;
  curPathIndex = 0;

  //get the current velocity of the vehicle
  velocity = transform.forward;
}
```

There are only two methods that are important in this script—the `Update` and `Steer` methods. Let's take a look at the following code:

```
void Update () {
  //Unify the speed
  curSpeed = speed * Time.deltaTime;

  targetPoint = path.GetPoint(curPathIndex);

  //If reach the radius within the path then move to next
    //point in the path
      if (Vector3.Distance(transform.position, targetPoint) <
        path.Radius) {
        //Don't move the vehicle if path is finished
      if (curPathIndex < pathLength - 1) curPathIndex++;
        else if (isLooping) curPathIndex = 0;
        else return;
  }

  //Move the vehicle until the end point is reached in
    //the path
      if (curPathIndex >= pathLength ) return;

  //Calculate the next Velocity towards the path
      if (curPathIndex >= pathLength-1&& !isLooping)
        velocity += Steer(targetPoint, true);
        else velocity += Steer(targetPoint);

  //Move the vehicle according to the velocity
    transform.position += velocity;
  //Rotate the vehicle towards the desired Velocity
```

```
    transform.rotation = Quaternion.LookRotation(velocity);
}
```

In the `Update` method, we check whether our entity has reached a particular waypoint by calculating the distance between its current position and the path's radius range. If it's in the range, we increase the index to look it up from the waypoints array; in other words, we move our current destination to the next waypoint. If it was the last waypoint, we check the `isLooping` flag. If it is active, then we set the destination to the starting waypoint; otherwise, we stop. An alternative solution is to program it so that our object turns around and goes back the way it came. This is not a difficult task, so we'll leave this to the reader as a useful practice exercise.

In the next part, we calculate the acceleration from the `Steer` method in which we rotate our entity and update the position according to the speed and direction of the velocity:

```
//Steering algorithm to steer the vector towards the target
  public Vector3 Steer(Vector3 target,
    bool bFinalPoint = false) {
  //Calculate the directional vector from the current
    //position towards the target point
  Vector3 desiredVelocity = (target -transform.position);
  float dist = desiredVelocity.magnitude;

  //Normalise the desired Velocity
  desiredVelocity.Normalize();

  //Calculate the velocity according to the speed
  if (bFinalPoint&&dist<10.0f) desiredVelocity *=
    (curSpeed * (dist / 10.0f));
    else desiredVelocity *= curSpeed;

  //Calculate the force Vector
  Vector3 steeringForce = desiredVelocity - velocity;
  Vector3 acceleration = steeringForce / mass;

  return acceleration;
  }
}
```

The `Steer` method takes two parameters: the target position to move to, and a Boolean, telling us whether this is the final waypoint in the path or not. As first, we calculate the remaining distance from the current position to the target position. When we subtract the current position vector from the target position vector, we get a vector pointing toward the target position. The magnitude of this vector is the remaining distance. We are not interested in the vector's size, just in its direction, so we normalize it.

If the waypoint we are moving to is the final waypoint, and the distance is less than 10, we slow down the velocity gradually, until the velocity finally becomes zero and our character correctly stops in place. Otherwise, we update the target velocity with the desired speed value. In the same way as we did before, if we subtract the current velocity vector from this target velocity vector, we can calculate the new steering vector. Then, by dividing this vector by the mass value of our entity, we get the acceleration.

If you run the scene, you should see your cube object following the path. You can also see the path in the editor view. Play around with the speed and mass values of the follower and radius values of the path, and see how they affect the overall behavior of the system.

Avoiding obstacles

In this section, we will explore obstacle avoidance. As a first step, we need, of course, obstacles. We will set up a scene similar to the one shown in the following screenshot. Then, we will create a script for our character so that it can avoid the obstacles while trying to reach the target point. The algorithm presented here uses the raycasting method, which is very straightforward, but on the other hand, it can only avoid the obstacles that are blocking the path directly in front of it:

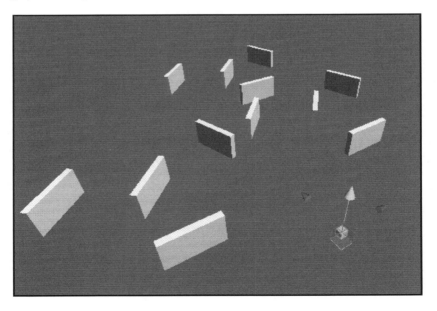

A sample scene setup

To create this, we make a few cube entities and group them under an empty game object called **Obstacles**. We will also create another cube object called `Agent` and give it our obstacle avoidance script. We will then create a ground plane object to assist in finding a target position:

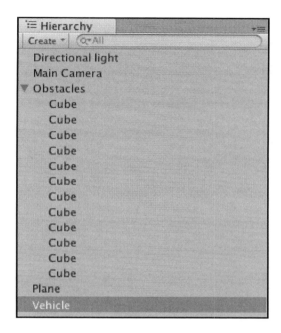

Here is how the Hierarchy is organized

It is worth noting that this `Agent` object is not a pathfinder; we only avoid obstacles locally. As such, if we set too many walls up, the `Agent` might have a hard time finding the target: for instance, if the `Agent` ends up facing a dead end in a U-shaped object, it may not be able to get out. Try a few different wall setups and see how our `Agent` performs.

Adding a custom layer

We will now add a custom layer to the obstacles object:

1. To add a new layer, we will navigate to **Edit** | **Project Settings** | **Tags**:

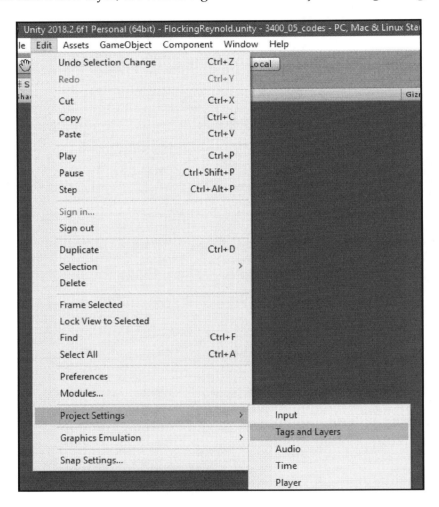

2. Assign the name Obstacles to **User Layer 8**.

3. We then go back to our cube entity and set its `layer` property to `Obstacles`:

Creating a new layer

4. When we use raycasting to detect obstacles, we check for those entities, but only on this particular layer. This way, the physics system can ignore objects hit by a ray that are not obstacles, such as bushes or vegetation:

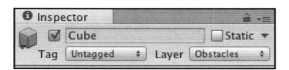

Assigning our new layer

5. For larger projects, our game objects probably already have a layer assigned to them. As such, instead of changing the object's layer to `Obstacles`, we would instead make a list of layers for our cube entity to use when detecting obstacles. We will talk more about this in the next section.

 Layers are most commonly used by cameras to render a part of the scene, and by lights to illuminate only some parts of the scene. But they can also be used by raycasting to selectively ignore colliders or to create collisions. You can learn more about this at
https://docs.unity3d.com/Manual/Layers.html.

Obstacle avoidance

Now, it is time to make the script that makes our cube entity avoid the walls:

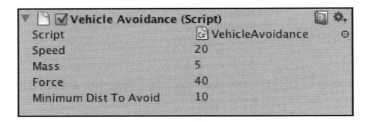

Properties of our Vehicle Avoidance script

As usual, we first initialize our entity script with the default properties and draw GUI text in our OnGUI method. Let's take a look at the following code in the VehicleAvoidance.cs file:

```
using UnityEngine;
using System.Collections;

public class VehicleAvoidance : MonoBehaviour {
  public float speed = 20.0f;
  public float mass = 5.0f;
  public float force = 50.0f;
  public float minimumDistToAvoid = 20.0f;

  //Actual speed of the vehicle
  private float curSpeed;
  private Vector3 targetPoint;

  // Use this for initialization
  void Start () {
    mass = 5.0f;
    targetPoint = Vector3.zero;
  }

  void OnGUI () {
    GUILayout.Label("Click anywhere to move the vehicle.");
  }
```

Then, in the Update method, we update the agent entity's position and rotation based on the direction vector returned by the AvoidObstacles method:

```
//Update is called once per frame
void Update () {
```

```
//Vehicle move by mouse click
RaycastHit hit;
var ray = Camera.main.ScreenPointToRay
    (Input.mousePosition);

if (Input.GetMouseButtonDown(0) &&
  Physics.Raycast(ray, out hit, 100.0f)) {
  targetPoint = hit.point;
}

//Directional vector to the target position
Vector3 dir = (targetPoint - transform.position);
dir.Normalize();

//Apply obstacle avoidance
AvoidObstacles(ref dir);

//...

}
```

The first thing we do in the `Update` method is retrieve the mouse-click position so that we can move our character. We do this by shooting a ray from the camera in the direction it's facing. Then, we take the point where the ray hits the ground plane as the target position. Once we get the target position vector, we can calculate the direction vector by subtracting the current position vector from the target position vector. Then, we call the `AvoidObstacles` method and pass in this direction vector:

```
//Calculate the new directional vector to avoid
  //the obstacle
public void AvoidObstacles(ref Vector3 dir) {
  RaycastHit hit;

  //Only detect layer 8 (Obstacles)
  int layerMask = 1<<8;

  //Check that the vehicle hit with the obstacles within
    //it's minimum distance to avoid
  if (Physics.Raycast(transform.position,
    transform.forward, out hit,
    minimumDistToAvoid, layerMask)) {
  //Get the normal of the hit point to calculate the
    //new direction
    Vector3 hitNormal = hit.normal;
    hitNormal.y = 0.0f; //Don't want to move in Y-Space

    //Get the new directional vector by adding force to
```

```
        //vehicle's current forward vector
        dir = transform.forward + hitNormal * force;
      }
    }
  }
```

The AvoidObstacles method is also quite simple. The only trick to note here is that raycasting interacts selectively with the Obstacles layer that we specified at **User Layer 8** in our Unity3D Tag Manager. The Raycast method accepts a layer mask parameter to determine which layers to ignore and which to consider during raycasting. Now, if you look at how many layers you can specify in Tag Manager, you'll find a total of 32 layers. Therefore, Unity3D uses a 32-bit integer number to represent this layer mask parameter. For example, the following would represent a zero in 32 bits:

```
0000 0000 0000 0000 0000 0000 0000 0000
```

By default, Unity3D uses the first eight layers as built-in layers. So, when you raycast without using a layer mask parameter, it'll raycast against all those eight layers, which could be represented in a bitmask, as follows:

```
0000 0000 0000 0000 0000 0000 1111 1111
```

Our Obstacles layer was set at layer 8 (9th index), and we only want to raycast against this layer. So, we'd like to set up our bitmask in the following way:

```
0000 0000 0000 0000 0000 0001 0000 0000
```

The easiest way to set up this bitmask is by using the bit shift operators. We only need to place the on bit, 1, at the 9th index, which means we can just move that bit 8 places to the left. So, we use the left shift operator to move the bit 8 places to the left, as shown in the following code:

```
int layerMask = 1<<8;
```

If we wanted to use multiple layer masks, say, layer 8 and layer 9, an easy way would be to use the bitwise OR operator, as follows:

```
int layerMask = (1<<8) | (1<<9);
```

You can also find a good discussion on using layer masks on Unity3D online. The question and answer site can be found at http://answers.unity3d.com/questions/8715/how-do-i-use-layermasks.html.

Once we have the layer mask, we call the `Physics.Raycast` method from the current entity's position and in the forward direction. For the length of the ray, we use the `minimumDistToAvoid` variable, so that we only avoid those obstacles that are hit by the ray within this distance.

Then, we take the normal vector of the hit ray, multiply it with the force vector, and add it to the current direction of the entity to get the new resultant direction vector, which we return from this method:

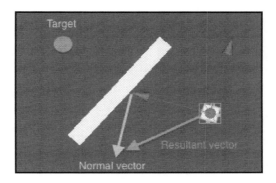

How our cube entity avoids a wall

Then, in the `Update` method, we use this new direction to rotate the AI entity and update the position according to the speed value:

```
void Update () {

    //...

    //Don't move the vehicle when the target point
      //is reached
    if (Vector3.Distance(targetPoint,
      transform.position) < 3.0f) return;

      //Assign the speed with delta time
      curSpeed = speed * Time.deltaTime;

      //Rotate the vehicle to its target
        //directional vector
    var rot = Quaternion.LookRotation(dir);
    transform.rotation = Quaternion.Slerp
      (transform.rotation, rot, 5.0f *
      Time.deltaTime);

      //Move the vehicle towards
```

```
transform.position += transform.forward *
    curSpeed;
}
```

Summary

In this chapter, we set up two scenes and studied how to build path-following agents with obstacle avoidance behavior. We learned about the Unity3D layer feature and how to selectively raycast against a particular layer. Although these examples were simple, we can apply these simple techniques to various scenarios. For instance, we can set up a path along a road, and by using some vehicle models combined with obstacle avoidance behavior, we can easily set up a decent traffic simulation. Alternatively, you could just replace them with biped characters and build a crowd simulation. You can also combine them with some finite state machines to add more behaviors and make them more intelligent. The simple obstacle avoidance behavior that we implemented in this chapter doesn't consider the optimal path to reach the target position. Instead, it just goes straight to that target, and only if an obstacle is seen within a particular distance does it try to avoid it. It's supposed to be used among moving or dynamic objects and obstacles.

In the following chapter, we'll study how to implement a pathfinding algorithm, called A*, to determine the optimal path before moving, while still avoiding static obstacles.

7
A* Pathfinding

In this chapter, we, implement the A* algorithm in Unity3D using C#. The A* pathfinding algorithm is widely used in games and interactive applications because of its simplicity and effectiveness. We talked about this algorithm previously in `Chapter 1`, *Introduction to AI*. However, here, we'll review the algorithm again, this time from an implementation perspective.

In this chapter, we will look at the following topics:

- Revisiting the A* algorithm
- Implementing the A* algorithm
- Setting up the scene
- Testing the pathfinder

Revisiting the A* algorithm

Let's review the A* algorithm again, before we proceed to implement it in the next section. The foundation of any pathfinding algorithm is a representation of the world. Pathfinding algorithms cannot search over the noisy structure of polygons in the game map; instead, we need to provide them with a simplified version of the world in which we identify the locations that can be traversed by the agent, and the ones that are inaccessible.

There are many ways of doing this; however, for this example, we will use one of the most straightforward solutions: a 2D grid. Therefore, we will implement the `GridManager` class in order to convert the real map into a 2D tile representation. The `GridManager` class keeps a list of `Node` objects, representing a single tile in the 2D grid. Of course, we need to implement the `Node` class too: this class stores node information such as its position, whether it's a traversable node or an obstacle, the cost to pass through, the cost to reach the target `Node`, and so on.

Once we have a world representation, we implement an `AStar` class for the actual A* pathfinding algorithm. The class is very simple; all the hard work is concentrated on the `FindPath` method. The class has two variables to store the nodes that have been visited and the nodes that we are going to explore. We call these variables closed list and open list, respectively. We implement the open lists as a `PriorityQueue` class, because we want to be able to get the `Node` with the lower score as fast as possible. The closed list, instead, wants a data structure that allows us to check if a `Node` is already contained in the list: usually, any set data structure is a good choice.

Finally, the A* pseudocode is outlined here:

1. First, the algorithm takes the starting node and puts it in the open list.
2. As long as the open list is not empty, the algorithm proceeds to perform the following steps.
3. It picks the first node from the open list and defines it as the current node (of course, we are assuming that we are using `PriorityQueues` for the open list).
4. Then, it gets the neighboring nodes of this current node, excluding obstacle types (such as a wall or canyon that can't be passed through). This step is usually called *expansion*.
5. For each neighbor node in step 4, it checks if it is already in the closed list. If not, it calculates the total cost (F) for this neighbor node using the following formula:

   F = G + H

   Here, G is the total cost from the starting node to this node (usually computed by adding the cost of moving from parent to neighbor to the G value of the parent node), and H is the estimated total cost from this node to the final target node. We will go over the problem of estimating the cost in later sections.

6. The algorithm stores that cost data in the neighbor node object, and it assigns the current node as the neighbor's parent node. Later, we will use this parent node data to trace back from the end node, reconstructing the actual path.
7. It put this neighbor node in the open list. The open list is a priority queue ordered by the F value; therefore, the first node in the open list is always the one with the lowest F value.
8. If there are no more neighbor nodes to process, the algorithm puts the current node in the closed list and removes it from the open list.
9. The algorithm goes back to step 2.

Once you have completed this algorithm, if there's an obstacle-free path to reach the target node from the start node, then your current node is in the target node position. Otherwise, this means that there's no available path to the target node from the current node position.

When we get a valid path, we then have to trace back from the current node using the parent pointer until we reach the start node again. This gives us a path list of all the nodes that we chose during our pathfinding process, ordered from the target node to the start node. As a final step, we just reverse this path list and get the path in the right order.

Next, we're going to implement A* in Unity3D using C#. So, let's get started.

Implementing the A* algorithm

As a first step, we will implement the preliminary classes that we introduced before, such as the Node class, the GridManager class, and the PriorityQueue class. Then, we will use them in the main AStar class.

Node

The Node class will handle each tile object in our 2D grid and will be, used to represent the maps shown in the Node.cs file:

```
using UnityEngine;
using System.Collections;
using System;

public class Node : IComparable {
  public float nodeTotalCost;
  public float estimatedCost;
  public bool bObstacle;
  public Node parent;
  public Vector3 position;

  public Node() {
    this.estimatedCost = 0.0f;
    this.nodeTotalCost = 1.0f;
    this.bObstacle = false;
    this.parent = null;
  }

  public Node(Vector3 pos) {
    this.estimatedCost = 0.0f;
    this.nodeTotalCost = 1.0f;
```

```
      this.bObstacle = false;
      this.parent = null;
      this.position = pos;
   }

   public void MarkAsObstacle() {
      this.bObstacle = true;
   }
```

The Node class stores properties such as the cost from the starting point and the estimated cost to the end (G and H), flags to mark whether it is an obstacle, its positions, and its parent node. The nodeTotalCost is G, which is the movement cost value from the starting node to this node so far, and the estimatedCost is H, which is the total estimated cost from this node to the target node. We also have two simple constructor methods and a wrapper method to set, depending on whether this node is an obstacle or not. Then, we implement the CompareTo method, as shown in the following code:

```
   public int CompareTo(object obj) {
      Node node = (Node)obj;
      //Negative value means object comes before this in the sort
        //order.
      if (this.estimatedCost < node.estimatedCost)
        return -1;
      //Positive value means object comes after this in the sort
        //order.
      if (this.estimatedCost > node.estimatedCost) return 1;
      return 0;
   }
}
```

This method is important. Our Node class inherits from IComparable and we want to override the default CompareTo method. This new comparison function will be used when we need to sort the open list in our PriorityQueue implementation. The ArrayList type has a method called Sort, which basically looks for a CompareTo method implementation inside the object (in this case, the Node objects) in the list. Overriding CompareTo allows us to decide how a node is *greater than* another node. In our case, we want to sort the node objects based on our estimatedCost value.

You can learn more about the IComparable.CompareTo method, as a feature of the .NET framework, at http://msdn.microsoft.com/en-us/library/system.icomparable.compareto.aspx.

PriorityQueue

A `PriorityQueue` is an ordered data structure that's designed in such a way that the first element (the head) of the list is always the smallest or largest element (depending on the implementation). We will use this data structure to handle the nodes in the open list because we need to find the node with the smallest F value efficiently. The code for this is shown in the following `PriorityQueue.cs` class:

```
using UnityEngine;
using System.Collections;

public class PriorityQueue {
  private ArrayList nodes = new ArrayList();

  public int Length {
    get { return this.nodes.Count; }
  }

  public bool Contains(object node) {
    return this.nodes.Contains(node);
  }

  public Node First() {
    if (this.nodes.Count > 0) {
      return (Node)this.nodes[0];
    }
    return null;
  }

  public void Push(Node node) {
    this.nodes.Add(node);
    this.nodes.Sort();
  }

  public void Remove(Node node) {
    this.nodes.Remove(node);
    //Ensure the list is sorted
    this.nodes.Sort();
  }
}
```

This code should be easy enough to understand. One thing to notice is that after adding or removing the node from the internal list, we call the `Sort` method. This, in turn, calls the `Node` object's `CompareTo` method, and sorts the nodes accordingly by the `estimatedCost` value.

The GridManager class

A `GridManager` class handles the 2D grid representation for the world map. We keep it as a singleton instance of the `GridManager` class, as we only need one object to represent the map. A singleton is a programming pattern that restricts the instantiation of a class to one object and, therefore, it makes the instance easily accessible from any point of the application. The steps to set up the `GridManager` are as follows:

1. The code for setting up the `GridManager` is shown in the following `GridManager.cs` file:

```
using UnityEngine;
using System.Collections;

public class GridManager : MonoBehaviour {
  private static GridManager s_Instance = null;

  public static GridManager instance {
    get {
      if (s_Instance == null) {
        s_Instance = FindObjectOfType(typeof(GridManager))
          as GridManager;
        if (s_Instance == null)
          Debug.Log("Could not locate a GridManager " +
            "object. \n You have to have exactly " +
            "one GridManager in the scene.");
      }
      return s_Instance;
    }
  }
}
```

2. We look for the `GridManager` object in the scene and, if found, we keep it in the `s_Instance` static variable:

```
public int numOfRows;
public int numOfColumns;
public float gridCellSize;
public bool showGrid = true;
public bool showObstacleBlocks = true;

private Vector3 origin = new Vector3();
private GameObject[] obstacleList;
public Node[,] nodes { get; set; }
public Vector3 Origin {
  get { return origin; }
}
```

3. We declare all the variables that we need to represent our map: the number of rows and columns; the size of each grid tile; and the Boolean variables for visualizing the grid and obstacles; and storing all the nodes present in the grid. The final product is shown in the following code:

```
void Awake() {
  obstacleList = GameObject.FindGameObjectsWithTag("Obstacle");
  CalculateObstacles();
}
// Find all the obstacles on the map
void CalculateObstacles() {
  nodes = new Node[numOfColumns, numOfRows];
  int index = 0;
  for (int i = 0; i < numOfColumns; i++) {
    for (int j = 0; j < numOfRows; j++) {
      Vector3 cellPos = GetGridCellCenter(index);
      Node node = new Node(cellPos);
      nodes[i, j] = node;
      index++;
    }
  }
  if (obstacleList != null && obstacleList.Length > 0) {
    //For each obstacle found on the map, record it in our list
    foreach (GameObject data in obstacleList) {
      int indexCell = GetGridIndex(data.transform.position);
      int col = GetColumn(indexCell);
      int row = GetRow(indexCell);
      nodes[row, col].MarkAsObstacle();
    }
  }
}
```

4. In the code, we look for all the game objects with the Obstacle tag and put them in the obstacleList.

5. Then, we set up the 2D array for the nodes in the CalculateObstacles method:
   1. First, we just create the node objects with default properties.
   2. After that, we examine our obstacleList. For each one of them, we identify all of the grid's row and column values that are occupied by the obstacle, and we set the corresponding nodes to be obstacles.

The `GridManager` has a couple of helper methods to traverse the grid and get the grid cell data. We show some of them in the following list, with a brief description of what they do. The implementation is simple, so we won't go into too much detail:

- The `GetGridCellCenter` method returns the position of the grid cell in world coordinates from the cell index, as shown in the following code:

```
public Vector3 GetGridCellCenter(int index) {
  Vector3 cellPosition = GetGridCellPosition(index);
  cellPosition.x += (gridCellSize / 2.0f);
  cellPosition.z += (gridCellSize / 2.0f);
  return cellPosition;
}

public Vector3 GetGridCellPosition(int index) {
  int row = GetRow(index);
  int col = GetColumn(index);
  float xPosInGrid = col * gridCellSize;
  float zPosInGrid = row * gridCellSize;
  return Origin + new Vector3(xPosInGrid, 0.0f, zPosInGrid);
}
```

- The `GetGridIndex` method returns the grid cell index in the grid from the given position:

```
public int GetGridIndex(Vector3 pos) {
  if (!IsInBounds(pos)) {
    return -1;
  }
  pos -= Origin;
  int col = (int)(pos.x / gridCellSize);
  int row = (int)(pos.z / gridCellSize);
  return (row * numOfColumns + col);
}

public bool IsInBounds(Vector3 pos) {
  float width = numOfColumns * gridCellSize;
  float height = numOfRows* gridCellSize;
  return (pos.x >= Origin.x &&  pos.x <= Origin.x + width &&
      pos.x <= Origin.z + height && pos.z >= Origin.z);
}
```

- The `GetRow` and `GetColumn` methods return the row and column data of the grid cell from the given index:

```
public int GetRow(int index) {
  int row = index / numOfColumns;
  return row;
}

public int GetColumn(int index) {
  int col = index % numOfColumns;
  return col;
}
```

- Another important method is `GetNeighbours`, which is used by the `AStar` class to retrieve the neighboring nodes of a particular node:

```
public void GetNeighbours(Node node, ArrayList neighbors) {
  Vector3 neighborPos = node.position;
  int neighborIndex = GetGridIndex(neighborPos);

  int row = GetRow(neighborIndex);
  int column = GetColumn(neighborIndex);

  //Bottom
  int leftNodeRow = row - 1;
  int leftNodeColumn = column;
  AssignNeighbour(leftNodeRow, leftNodeColumn, neighbors);

  //Top
  leftNodeRow = row + 1;
  leftNodeColumn = column;
  AssignNeighbour(leftNodeRow, leftNodeColumn, neighbors);

  //Right
  leftNodeRow = row;
  leftNodeColumn = column + 1;
  AssignNeighbour(leftNodeRow, leftNodeColumn, neighbors);

  //Left
  leftNodeRow = row;
  leftNodeColumn = column - 1;
  AssignNeighbour(leftNodeRow, leftNodeColumn, neighbors);
}

void AssignNeighbour(int row, int column, ArrayList neighbors) {
  if (row != -1 && column != -1 &&
      row < numOfRows && column < numOfColumns) {
    Node nodeToAdd = nodes[row, column];
```

```
      if (!nodeToAdd.bObstacle) {
        neighbors.Add(nodeToAdd);
      }
    }
  }
```

Here, we first retrieve the neighboring nodes of the current node in the left, right, top, and bottom directions. Then, inside the `AssignNeighbour` method, we check the node to see whether it's an obstacle. If it's not, then we push that neighbor node to the referenced array list, `neighbors`.

- The following method is a debug aid method which is used to visualize the grid and obstacle blocks:

```
void OnDrawGizmos() {
  if (showGrid) {
    DebugDrawGrid(transform.position, numOfRows, numOfColumns,
        gridCellSize, Color.blue);
  }
  Gizmos.DrawSphere(transform.position, 0.5f);
  if (showObstacleBlocks) {
    Vector3 cellSize = new Vector3(gridCellSize, 1.0f,
      gridCellSize);
    if (obstacleList != null && obstacleList.Length > 0) {
      foreach (GameObject data in obstacleList) {
        Gizmos.DrawCube(GetGridCellCenter(
            GetGridIndex(data.transform.position)), cellSize);
      }
    }
  }
}

public void DebugDrawGrid(Vector3 origin, int numRows, int
  numCols,float cellSize, Color color) {
  float width = (numCols * cellSize);
  float height = (numRows * cellSize);

  // Draw the horizontal grid lines
  for (int i = 0; i < numRows + 1; i++) {
    Vector3 startPos = origin + i * cellSize * new Vector3(0.0f,
      0.0f, 1.0f);
    Vector3 endPos = startPos + width * new Vector3(1.0f, 0.0f,
      0.0f);
    Debug.DrawLine(startPos, endPos, color);
  }

  // Draw the vertial grid lines
```

```
for (int i = 0; i < numCols + 1; i++) {
    Vector3 startPos = origin + i * cellSize * new Vector3(1.0f,
        0.0f, 0.0f);
    Vector3 endPos = startPos + height * new Vector3(0.0f, 0.0f,
        1.0f);
    Debug.DrawLine(startPos, endPos, color);
  }
 }
}
```

Gizmos can be used to draw visual debugging and setup aids inside the editor scene view. OnDrawGizmos is called every frame by the engine. So, if the debug flags, showGrid and showObstacleBlocks, are checked, we just draw the grid with lines and obstacle cube objects with cubes. We won't go through the DebugDrawGrid method, as it's quite simple.

You can learn more about gizmos in the following Unity3D reference documentation at https://docs.unity3d.com/ScriptReference/Gizmos.html.

The AStar class

The AStar class implements the pathfinding algorithm using the classes we have implemented so far. If you want a quick review of the A* algorithm, see the *Revisiting the A* algorithm* section from earlier in this chapter. The steps for implementation of AStar are as follows:

1. We start with our openList declaration, which is a PriorityQueue type variable, and closedList, which is a HashSet of nodes. The AStar.cs file is as follows:

    ```
    using UnityEngine;
    using System.Collections;
    using System.Collections.Generic;

    public class AStar {
        public static PriorityQueue openList;
        public static HashSet<Node> closedList;
    ```

2. We implement a method called `HeuristicEstimateCost` to calculate the cost between the two nodes. The calculation is simple. We just find the direction vector between the two by subtracting one position vector from another. The magnitude of this resultant vector gives the direct distance from the current node to the target node:

```
private static float HeuristicEstimateCost(Node curNode,
    Node goalNode) {
  Vector3 vecCost = curNode.position - goalNode.position;
  return vecCost.magnitude;
}
```

In theory, you can replace this function with any function, returning the distance between `curNode` and `goalNode`. However, in order for A* to return the shortest possible path, this function must be *admissible*. In short, an admissible heuristic function is a function that never overestimates the real cost between `curNode` and `goalNode`. As an exercise, you can easily verify that the preceding function is admissible. For more information on heuristic functions, you can visit https://theory.stanford.edu/~amitp/GameProgramming/Heuristics.html.

3. We have the main `FindPath` method:

```
public static ArrayList FindPath(Node start, Node goal) {
  openList = new PriorityQueue();
  openList.Push(start);
  start.nodeTotalCost = 0.0f;
  start.estimatedCost = HeuristicEstimateCost(start, goal);

  closedList = new HashSet<Node>();
  Node node = null;
```

4. In the following snippet, we initialize the open and closed lists. Starting with the start node, we put it in our open list. Then, we start processing our open list:

```
while (openList.Length != 0) {
  node = openList.First();
  //Check if the current node is the target node
  if (node.position == goal.position) {
    return CalculatePath(node);
  }

  //Create an ArrayList to store the neighboring nodes
  ArrayList neighbours = new ArrayList();

  GridManager.instance.GetNeighbours(node, neighbours);
```

```
for (int i = 0; i < neighbours.Count; i++) {
    Node neighbourNode = (Node)neighbours[i];

    if (!closedList.Contains(neighbourNode)) {
        float cost = HeuristicEstimateCost(node,
            neighbourNode);

        float totalCost = node.nodeTotalCost + cost;
        float neighbourNodeEstCost = HeuristicEstimateCost(
            neighbourNode, goal);

        neighbourNode.nodeTotalCost = totalCost;
        neighbourNode.parent = node;
        neighbourNode.estimatedCost = totalCost +
            neighbourNodeEstCost;

        if (!openList.Contains(neighbourNode)) {
            openList.Push(neighbourNode);
        }
    }
}
//Add the current node to the closed list
closedList.Add(node);
//and remove it from openList
openList.Remove(node);
}

if (node.position != goal.position) {
    Debug.LogError("Goal Not Found");
    return null;
}
return CalculatePath(node);
}
```

5. The following code implementation strictly follows the algorithm that we have discussed previously, so you can refer back to it if something is not clear:
    1. Get the first node from our `openList`. Remember, the `openList` is always sorted in increasing order. Therefore, the first node is always the node with the lowest F value.
    2. Check if the current node is already at the target node. If so, exit the `while` loop and build the `path` array.

3. Create an array list to store the neighboring nodes of the current node being processed. Use the GetNeighbours method to retrieve the neighbors from the grid.

4. For every node in the neighbors array, we check if it's already in the closedList. If not, we calculate the cost values, update the node properties with the new cost values and the parent node data, and put it in the openList.

5. Push the current node to the closedList and remove it from openList. Go back to step 1.

If there are no more nodes in the openList, the current node should be at the target node if there's a valid path available.

6. Then, we just call the CalculatePath method with the current node parameter:

```
private static ArrayList CalculatePath(Node node) {
  ArrayList list = new ArrayList();
  while (node != null) {
    list.Add(node);
    node = node.parent;
  }
  list.Reverse();
  return list;
}
}
```

The CalculatePath method traces through each node's parent node object and builds an array list. Since we want a path array from the start node to the target node, we just call the Reverse method.

Now, we'll write a test script to test this, and set up a demo scene.

The TestCode class

The TestCode class will use the AStar class to find the path from the start node to the target node, as shown in the following code from the TestCode.cs file:

```
using UnityEngine;
using System.Collections;

public class TestCode : MonoBehaviour {
  private Transform startPos, endPos;
  public Node startNode { get; set; }
```

```
public Node goalNode { get; set; }

public ArrayList pathArray;

GameObject objStartCube, objEndCube;
private float elapsedTime = 0.0f;
//Interval time between pathfinding
public float intervalTime = 1.0f;
```

In the preceding snippet, we first set up the variables that we need to reference. The
pathArray variable stores the nodes array that's returned from the AStar FindPath
method.

In the following code block, we use the Start method to look for objects with the
tags Start and End, and initialize the pathArray as well. We are trying to find a new path
at every interval, specified by the intervalTime property, in case the positions of the start
and end nodes have changed. Finally, we call the FindPath method:

```
void Start () {
  objStartCube = GameObject.FindGameObjectWithTag("Start");
  objEndCube = GameObject.FindGameObjectWithTag("End");

  pathArray = new ArrayList();
  FindPath();
}

void Update () {
  elapsedTime += Time.deltaTime;
  if (elapsedTime >= intervalTime) {
    elapsedTime = 0.0f;
    FindPath();
  }
}
```

Since we implemented our pathfinding algorithm in the AStar class, finding a path is now
a lot simpler. In the following snippet, we first take the positions of the start and end game
objects. Then, we create new Node objects using the GetGridIndex helper methods
in GridManager to calculate their respective row and column index positions inside the
grid. After that, we call the AStar.FindPath method with the start node and target node,
and store the returned array list in the local pathArray property. Finally, we implement
the OnDrawGizmos method to draw and visualize the path that's found:

```
void FindPath() {
  startPos = objStartCube.transform;
  endPos = objEndCube.transform;
```

```
startNode = new Node(GridManager.instance.GetGridCellCenter(
    GridManager.instance.GetGridIndex(startPos.position)));

goalNode = new Node(GridManager.instance.GetGridCellCenter(
    GridManager.instance.GetGridIndex(endPos.position)));

pathArray = AStar.FindPath(startNode, goalNode);
}
```

We look through our `pathArray` and use the `Debug.DrawLine` method to draw the lines, connecting the nodes in the `pathArray`:

```
void OnDrawGizmos() {
  if (pathArray == null)
    return;

  if (pathArray.Count > 0) {
    int index = 1;
    foreach (Node node in pathArray) {
      if (index < pathArray.Count) {
        Node nextNode = (Node)pathArray[index];
        Debug.DrawLine(node.position, nextNode.position,
          Color.green);
        index++;
      }
    }
  }
}
}
```

With that, when we run and test our program, we should be able to see a green line connecting the nodes from start to end. This is the found path.

Setting up the scene

We are going to set up a scene that looks like the following screenshot:

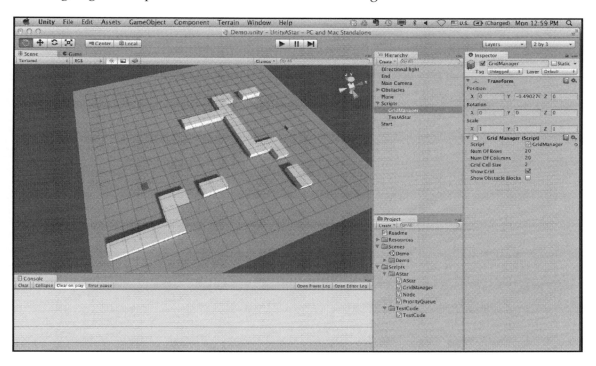

Our sample test scene with obstacles

Let's follow a step-by-step procedure to do this:

1. We will create a directional light, the start and end game objects, a few obstacle objects, a plane entity to be used as ground, and two empty game objects in which we put the **GridManager** and **TestAStar** scripts. After this step, our scene hierarchy should be like this:

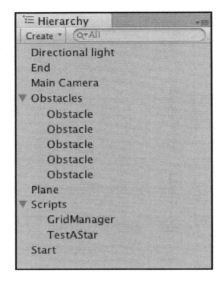

The demo scene hierarchy

2. We will create a bunch of cube entities and tag them as `Obstacle`. The `GridManager` will look for objects with this tag when it creates the grid world representation:

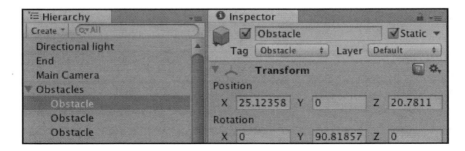

The Obstacle nodes seen in the inspector

3. We then create a cube entity and tag it as `Start`:

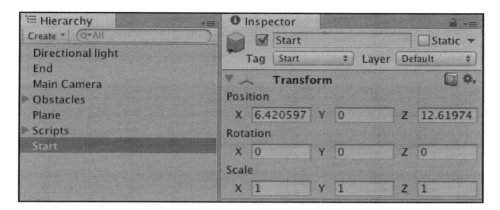

The Start node seen in the inspector

4. Then, we create another cube entity and tag it as `End`:

The End node seen in the inspector

5. We will create an empty game object and we will attach the `GridManager` script to it. We set the name as `GridManager` as well, because we use this name to look for the `GridManager` object from inside the other scripts.

6. In the inspector, we have to set up the number of rows and columns for the grid, as well as the size of each tile:

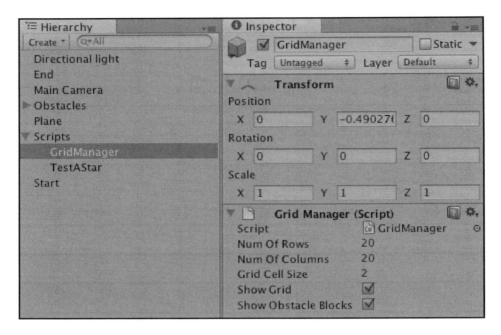

GridManager script

Testing the pathfinder

Once we hit the Play button, we should be able to see our A* pathfinding algorithm in action. By default, once you play the scene, Unity3D will switch to the **Game** view. Since our pathfinding visualization code draws in the debug editor view, to see the found path, you need to switch back to the **Scene** view or enable **Gizmos** visualization:

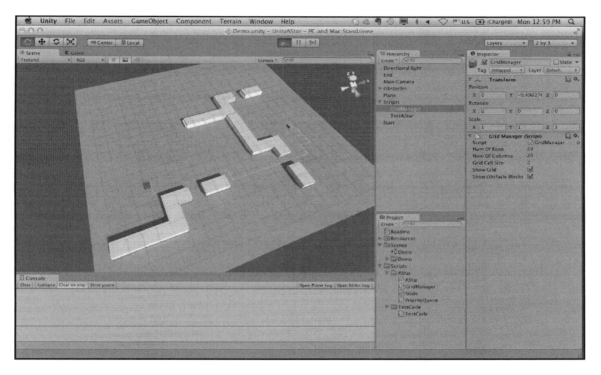

The first path found by the algorithm

Now, try to move the start or end node around in the scene using the editor's movement gizmo (not in the **Game** view, but the **Scene** view):

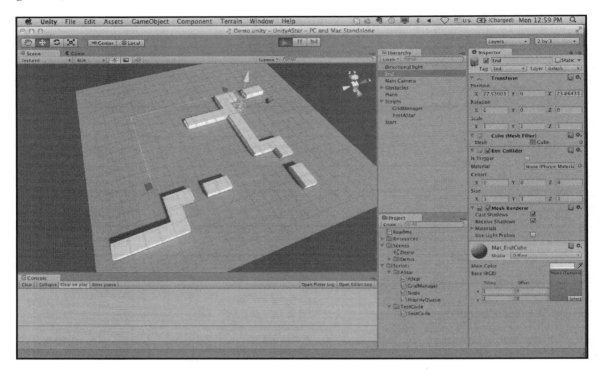

A second path found by the algorithm

You should see the path being updated dynamically in real time. If there is no available path, you will get an error message in the console window.

Summary

In this chapter, we learned how to implement the A* pathfinding algorithm in Unity3D. We implemented our own A* pathfinding class, as well as our grid class, priority queue class, and node class. We learned about the `IComparable` interface and how to override the `CompareTo` method to implement our custom ordering policy. We used debug draw functionalities to visualize the grid and path information.

In later chapters, we will see that with Unity3D's NavMesh and NavAgent features, it may not be necessary for you to implement a custom pathfinding algorithm on your own. Nonetheless, having an understanding of a basic pathfinding algorithm gives you a better foundation for getting to grips with many other advanced pathfinding techniques.

In the next chapter, we will look at how to extend the idea behind the A* algorithm as we look at navigation meshes.

8
Navigation Mesh

As we have seen in the previous chapter, the most important thing in pathfinding is the scene representation; the AI agents need to know where the obstacles are, especially static obstacles. Previously, we created our custom representation by dividing the map into a 2D grid, and then we implemented our custom pathfinding algorithm by implementing A* on that representation. Would it not be awesome if Unity could do all, that for us?

Fortunately, Unity can do this using NavMeshes. While in our 2D representation we divided the world into perfect squares, with NavMeshes, we divide the world using convex polygons. This representation has two interesting advantages: first, every polygon can be different from the other, and therefore we can use few a polygons for wide open areas and many smaller polygons for very crowded spaces; second, the agent is not locked on a grid, and so the pathfinding produces more natural paths.

In this chapter, we will see how we can use Unity's built-in **Navigation Meshes** (in short, NavMesh) generator to make pathfinding for AI agents much easier and more performant. Some years ago, NavMeshes were reserved for Unity's Pro users. Fortunately, this is not true anymore; NavMeshes are available in the free version of Unity!

The learning outcomes of this chapter are as follows:

- Setting up the map
- Building the scene with slopes
- Creating navigation areas
- An overview of Off Mesh links

Setting up the map

To get started, let's build a simple scene as, shown in the following screenshot. This is the first scene in the sample project, and is called `NavMesh01-Simple.scene`. You can use a plane as a ground object and several cube entities as the wall objects:

An image of the NavMesh01-Simple scene, a plane with obstacles

Navigation static

Once we add the floor and the obstacles, it is important to mark them as **Navigation Static** so that the NavMesh generator knows that those are the static objects to avoid. To do this, select all of the objects, click on the **Static** button, and choose **Navigation Static**, as shown in the following screenshot:

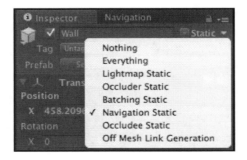

The Navigation Static property

Baking the navigation mesh

Now that we have completed the scene, let's bake the NavMesh. To do that, follow these steps:

1. We need to open the navigation window
2. Navigate to **Window** | **AI** | **Navigation**, and you should be able to see a window like this:

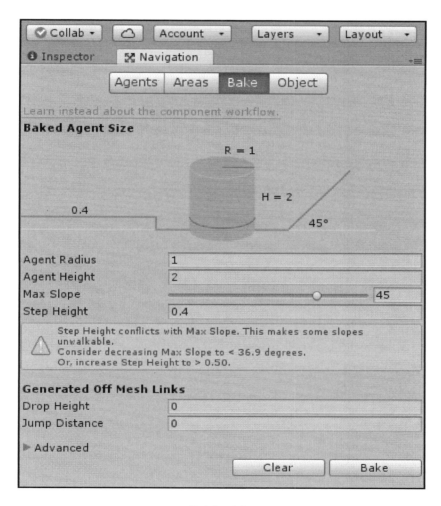

Navigation window

All the properties in the Navigation window are pretty much self-explanatory: the agent radius and height represent the size of the virtual agent used by Unity to bake the NavMesh; the Max Slope represents how much slope the character can walk; and so on. For more information, you can check out the following Unity reference documentation: `https://docs.unity3d.com/Manual/Navigation.html`.

3. For now, we will leave the default values and just click on **Bake**.

4. You should see a progress bar baking the NavMesh for your scene, and after a while, you will see the NavMesh in your scene, as shown in the following screenshot:

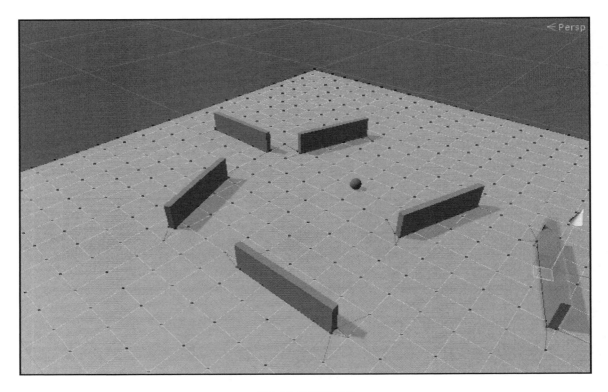

Navigation mesh being baked

NavMesh agent

We're pretty much done with setting up our super simple scene. Now, let's add some AI agents to see if it works:

1. We'll use our tank model here. If you're working with your own scene and don't have this model, you can just put a cube or a sphere entity as an agent. It'll work the same way:

Tank entity

2. Add the **Nav Mesh Agent** component to our tank entity. This component makes pathfinding really easy. We do not need to deal with implementing pathfinding algorithms such as A* anymore. By just setting the `destination` property of the component during runtime, our AI agent will automatically find the path itself.

3. Navigate to **Component** | **Navigation** | **Nav Mesh Agent** to add this component:

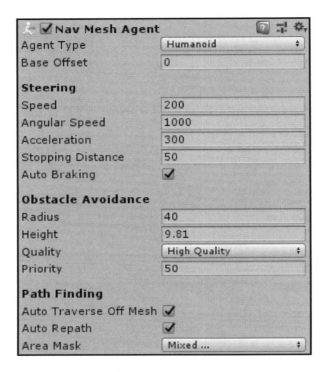

Nav Mesh Agent properties

 The Unity reference for the **Nav Mesh Agent** component can be found at `https://docs.unity3d.com/Manual/class-NavMeshAgent.html`.

One property to note is the `Area Mask` property. This specifies the NavMesh layers that this NavMesh agent can walk on. We will talk about navigation layers in the *Navigation Areas* section.

Updating an agents' destinations

Now that we have set up our AI agent, we need a way to tell this agent where to go and update the destination of the tanks to the mouse click position.

So, let's add a sphere entity, which is going to be used as a marker object, and then attach the `Target.cs` script to an empty game object. Drag and drop this sphere entity onto this script's `targetMarker` transform property in the inspector.

The Target.cs class

This is a simple class that does three things:

- Gets the mouse click position using a ray
- Updates the marker position
- Updates the destination property of all the NavMesh agents

The following lines show the code's that present in this class:

```
using UnityEngine;
using System.Collections;

public class Target : MonoBehaviour {
  private NavMeshAgent[] navAgents;
 public Transform targetMarker;

  void Start() {
    navAgents = FindObjectsOfType(typeof(NavMeshAgent)) as
        NavMeshAgent[];
  }

  void UpdateTargets(Vector3 targetPosition) {
    foreach (NavMeshAgent agent in navAgents) {
      agent.destination = targetPosition;
    }
  }

  void Update() {
    int button = 0;

    //Get the point of the hit position when the mouse is
    //being clicked
    if(Input.GetMouseButtonDown(button)) {
      Ray ray = Camera.main.ScreenPointToRay(
          Input.mousePosition);

      RaycastHit hitInfo;

      if (Physics.Raycast(ray.origin, ray.direction,
          out hitInfo)) {
```

```
        Vector3 targetPosition = hitInfo.point;
        UpdateTargets(targetPosition);
        targetMarker.position = targetPosition +
            new Vector3(0,5,0);
    }
  }
 }
}
```

At the start of the game, we look for all the NavMeshAgent type entities in our game and store them in our referenced NavMeshAgent array. Whenever there's a mouse click event, we do a simple raycast to determine the first objects that collide with our ray. If the ray hits any object, we update the position of our marker and update each NavMesh agent's destination by setting the destination property with the new position. We will be using this script throughout this chapter to tell the destination position for our AI agents.

Now, test run the scene, and click on a point where you want your tanks to go. The tanks should come as close as possible to that point, while avoiding every static obstacle (in this case, the walls).

Scene with slope

Let's build a scene with some slopes, like this:

Scene with slopes-NavMesh02-Slope.scene

One important thing to note is that the slopes and the wall should be in contact with each other. Objects need to be perfectly connected when creating such joins in the scene, with the purpose of generating a NavMesh later. Otherwise, there'll be gaps in the NavMesh, and the agents will not be able to find the path anymore. There's a feature called Off Mesh Link generation to solve this kind of problem. We will look at Off Mesh Links in the *Off Mesh Links* section later in this chapter. For now, let's concentrate on building the slope:

1. Make sure to connect the slope properly:

A well-connected slope

2. We can adjust the `Max Slope` property in the **Navigation** window's **Bake** tab according to the level of slope in our scenes that we want to allow the agents to travel. We'll use `45` degrees here. If your slopes are steeper than this, you can use a higher `Max Slope` value.

3. Bake the scene, and you should have a NavMesh generated, like this:

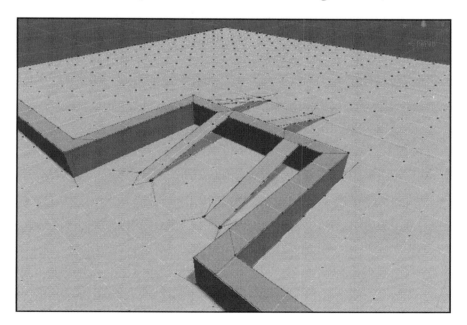

The generated Nav Mesh

4. We will place some tanks with the **Nav Mesh Agent** component.
5. Create a new cube object to be used as a target reference position.
6. We will be using our previous `Target.cs` script to update the destination property of the AI agent.
7. Test run the scene, and you should see the AI agent crossing the slopes to reach the target.

Navigation areas

In games with complex environments, we usually have some areas that are harder to traverse than others. For example, crossing a lake over the water is definitely harder than crossing it with a bridge. To simulate this, we want to make crossing the lake more costly than using a bridge. In this section, we will look at Navigation areas which are used as , a way to define different layers with different navigation cost values.

For this, we, build a scene, as shown in the following screenshot. There are three planes to represent two ground planes connected by a bridge-like structure, and a water plane between them. As you can see, crossing over the water plane is the most direct way to traverse the lake; however, passing through the water costs more than using the bridge and, therefore, the pathfinding algorithm will prefer the bridge over the water:

Scene with layers-NavMesh03-Layers.scene

Let's follow a step-by-step procedure so that we can create our own Navigation area:

1. Go to the **Navigation** window and select the **Areas** section:

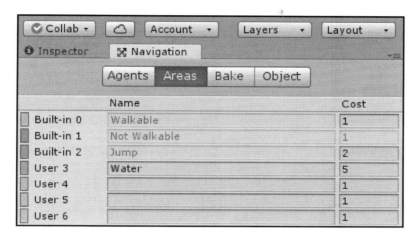

The Areas section in the Navigation window

 The Unity reference for NavMesh Areas can be found at `https://docs.unity3d.com/Manual/nav-AreasAndCosts.html`.

Unity comes with three default layers: `Default`, `Not Walkable`, and `Jump`, each with potentially different cost values.

2. Let's add a new layer called `Water` and give it a cost of 5.
3. Select the water plane.

4. Go to the **Navigation** window and under the **Object** tab, set **Navigation Area** to
   Water:

Water layer

5. Bake the NavMesh for the scene, and run it to test it.

You should see that the AI agents now choose the slope rather than going through the plane marked as the water layer because it's more expensive to choose that path. Try experimenting with placing the target object at different points in the water plane. You will see that the AI agents will sometimes swim back to the shore and take the bridge, rather than trying to swim all the way across the water.

Off Mesh Links

Sometimes, there may be some gaps in the scene that can make the navigation meshes disconnected. For example, our agents will not be able to find the path if our slopes are not connected to the walls in our previous examples. Or, we could have set up points where our agents could jump off the wall and onto the plane below. Unity has a feature called **Off Mesh Links** to connect such gaps. Off Mesh Links can either be set up manually or generated automatically by Unity's NavMesh generator.

Here's the example scene that we're going to build in this example. As you can see, there's a small gap between the two planes. Let's see how connect these two planes using Off Mesh Links:

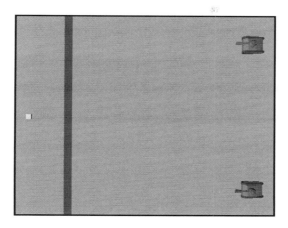

Scene with off mesh links-NavMesh04-OffMeshLinks.scene

Generated Off Mesh Links

Firstly, we will use autogenerated Off Mesh Links to connect the two planes. To do that, we need to follow these steps:

1. Mark these two planes as **Off Mesh Link Generation** static in the property inspector, as shown in the following screenshot:

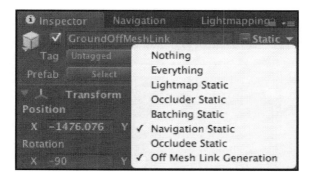

Off Mesh Link Generation static

2. Go to the **Navigation** window and notice the following properties under the **Bake** tab. You can set the distance threshold to autogenerate Off Mesh Links:

Generated Off Mesh Links properties

3. Click on **Bake**, and you should have Off Mesh Links connecting the two planes, like this:

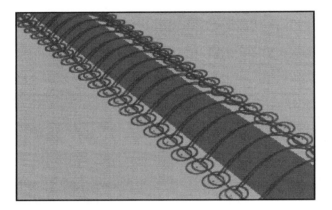

Generated Off Mesh Links

4. Now, our AI agents can traverse and find the path across both planes.

Agents will essentially be teleported to the other plane once they have reached the edge of the plane and found the Off Mesh Link. Of course, if teleporting agents are not what we want, we had better put a bridge in for the agents to cross.

Manual Off Mesh Links

If we don't want to generate Off Mesh Links along the edge, and we want to force the agents to come to a certain point to be teleported to another plane, we can also manually set up the Off Mesh Links. Here's how:

Manual Off Mesh Links setup

1. This is our scene with a significant gap between two planes. We placed two pairs of sphere entities on both sides of the plane.
2. Choose a sphere, and add an Off Mesh Link by navigating to **Component | Navigation | Off Mesh Link**.
3. We only need to add this component on one sphere.
4. Next, drag and drop the first sphere to the Start property, and the other sphere to the End property:

Off Mesh Link component

The Unity reference for Off Mesh Links can be found at `https://docs.unity3d.com/Manual/nav-CreateOffMeshLink.html`.

Manually generated Off Mesh Links

5. Go to the **Navigation** window and bake the scene.
6. The planes are now connected with the manual Off Mesh Links, which can be used by AI agents so that they can traverse, even though there's a gap.

Summary

In this chapter, we learned how to generate and use navigation meshes to represent the scene for pathfinding purposes. We studied how to set up different navigation layers with different costs for pathfinding. We used the **Nav Mesh Agent** component to find the path and move toward the target using the `destination` property. We set up Off Mesh Links to connect the gaps between the navigation meshes using both the autogeneration feature and a manual setup with the Off Mesh Link component.

With all this information, we can now easily create simple games with a fairly complicated AI. For example, you can try to set the destination property of AI tanks to the player's tank's position and make them follow it. Using simple FSMs, they can start attacking the player once they reach a certain distance. However, FSMs have taken us far, but they have their limits. In the next chapter, we will learn about Behavior Trees, and how they can be used to make AI decisions in even the most complex of games.

9
Behavior Trees

In a previous chapter, we saw a basic but effective way to implement and manage character states and behaviors: **Finite State Machines (FSMs)**. FSMs are simple to implement and very intuitive, but they have a fatal flaw: it is very hard to make them scale once states and transitions start getting numerous. For example, imagine a character that behaves differently depending on the amount of health and mana it has (high, medium, and low); we have a state when both health and mana are high, one in which, health is medium and, mana high, one in which they are both medium, and so on. In total, we have nine states just for that. If we add other conditions (such as player proximity, time of day, equipment, player's score, or whatever you may imagine), the number of states grows exponentially.

Luckily, we have a solution: **Behavior Trees (BTs)**. In essence, Behavior Trees are just another way to visualize complex FSMs, but they are fast, they provide reusability, and they are easy to maintain. Since their introduction in 2004 with Halo 2, they quickly became the preferred decision-making technique in games.

In this chapter, we will be doing the following:

- Exploring the basic principles of Behavior Trees, knowledge that you will be able to transfer to any BT plugin available for Unity (or other game engines)
- Implementing a small demo based on a popular free Unity plugin for Behavior Trees: **Behavior Bricks**

Introduction to Behavior Trees

A Behavior Tree is a hierarchical tree of Nodes that controls the flow of the AI character's behavior. When we execute a Node, the node can return three states: **success**, **failure**, or **running** (if the node's execution is spread over multiple frames, for instance, if it plays an animation). When the BT executor runs a tree, it starts from the root and starts executing every node in order, according to rules written in the nodes themselves.

A Node can be of three types:

- A **leaf** (a node without children)
- A **decorator** (a node with a single child)
- A **composite** node (a node with multiple children)

In general, **leaves** represent the **Action** that the characters can do or know (that is why they are commonly called an Action or Task); they may be actions such as `GoToTarget`, `OpenDoor`, `Jump`, or `TakeCover`, but also things like `IsObjectNear?` or `IsHealthLow?`. These actions depend on the character, the game, and the general game implementation.

A **decorator** is a node that modifies (decorates) the sub-tree under it. A common decorator is the `Negate` node. The node will invert the return value of the sub-tree; for instance, if the sub-tree returns `Success`, the decorator returns `Failure` and vice versa (of course, if the sub-tree returns `Running`, the decorator returns `Running` as well). Another common decorator is `Repeat`, a node that repeats its sub-tree a certain number of times.

A **composite node**, instead, represents a node with multiple children, and it is the most interesting case. There are two common composite nodes: `Sequence`, which runs all its children in order and returns `Success` if—and only if—all its children return success, and `Selector`, which tries to execute all its children in order but returns `Success` as soon as one of its children returns `Success`. However, many BT implementations contain many more composite nodes (such as nodes that run their children in parallel or according to some dynamic priority value; we will see an example of such a node in the demo).

Of course, this tree structure is not enough. Nodes need to exchange information with each other or with the game world. For instance, a `GoToTarget` node needs to know who the target is and where it is; an `IsObjectClose?` node needs to know to which object I am referring to and what distance I consider *close*. Naturally, we could write a `GoToX` node for each object in the game (`GoToTree01`, `GoToDoor23`, and so on), but you can easily imagine that this will become really messy very quickly.

For this reason, all the BT implementations contain a data structure called **Blackboard**. As in a physical real-life blackboard, every node can write and read data into it; for each node, we just need to specify where to look.

A simple example – patrolling robot

Let's look at this example (which we will later implement in Unity). Imagine a patrolling robot that shoots anything that gets near it, but works only during the daytime. A possible BT for this kind of agent is shown in the following diagram:

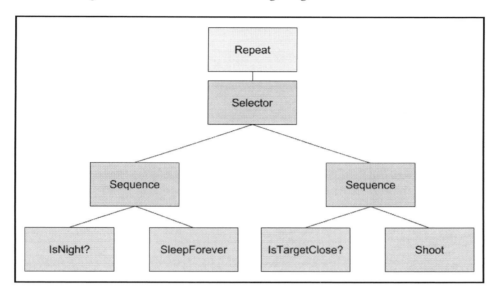

Let's run this BT, assuming that the target is close and it is not night:

1. The first node is a `Repeat` decorator; it does nothing but cycle the BTs, so we can ignore it for now.
2. The selector starts executing its first child; we go down to the left.
3. We are now at the first `Sequence` node; again, we execute the first node. `IsNight?` returns `Failure` (because it is not night!). Whenever one node returns `Failure`, the whole `Sequence` node returns `Failure`.
4. We traverse back up the tree to the `Selector`; now, we will go to the second branch.
5. Again, we execute `Sequence`.
6. This time, however, `IsTargetClose?` returns `Success`, so we can proceed to the next node, `Shoot`, which runs a game function that shows the projectile in the game.

The pattern of **Sequence | Condition | Action** is equivalent to if Condition is Success then Action. This pattern is so common that many BT implementations allow you to stack the Condition and the Action together. Therefore, we can rewrite the tree as follows:

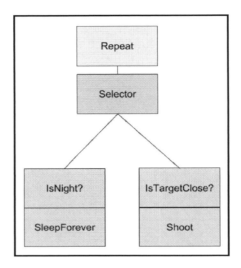

This tree is the same as the previous one.

Implementing a BT in Unity with Behavior Bricks

Behavior Bricks is a powerful but free Behavior Trees implementation for Unity developed by the Complutense University of Madrid in Spain. Using Behavior Bricks, you can start using BTs in your projects without the need to implement BTs from scratch. It also has a visual editor where you can drop and connect nodes without any additional code.

Follow these steps to install Behavior Bricks:

1. We need to go to the Unity Asset Store (**Window | General | Asset Store** or pressing *Ctrl + 9* in Windows or *Cmd + 9* on OSX).
2. Search for Behavior Bricks.
3. Download it and when that's done, we can import it in our project.

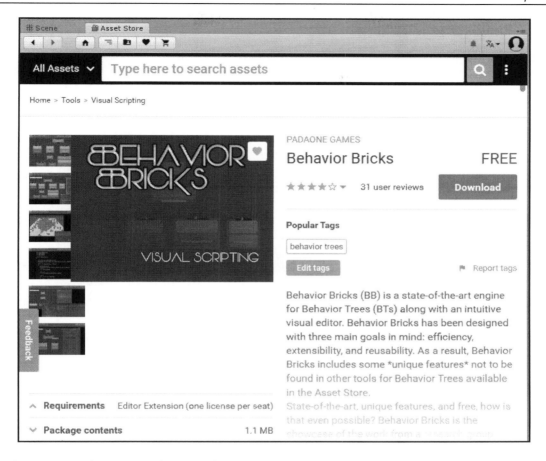

At this point, Behavior Bricks is ready to go and we can proceed with our demo.

The following steps will give you a brief idea of the steps to follow:

1. Set up the scene.
2. Implement a Day/Night cycle.
3. Design the Enemy Behavior.
4. Implement the Nodes.
5. Build the Tree.
6. Attach the BT to the Enemy.

Now, let's take a look at each of these steps individually.

Set up the scene

Let's follow a step-by-step process to do this:

1. We will start by adding our objects to the scene. We will add a big plane to the scene and we will call it *Floor* (you may also add a texture if you like; be creative as it will help you have fun with this simple demos).

2. We will add a sphere and a cube; we will call the sphere Player and the cube Enemy. In the enemy, we will add another empty object and we move it just outside the cube. We will call it shootPoint and it will be a placeholder for where the enemy shoots.

3. Then, place all these objects on the floor; you should have something similar to this:

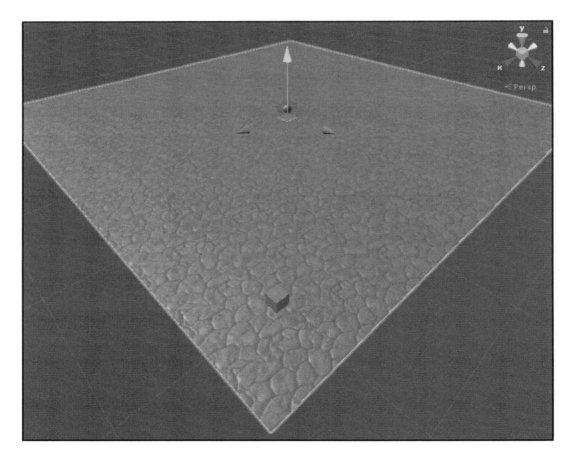

4. Now, because we want the player and the enemy to be able to move around, we need to create a NavMesh, just as we described in the previous chapter. Remember to add the NavMesh Agent component to both Player and Enemy!

5. Finally, if it is not present, add the **MainLight** tag to the Directional light.

Implement a Day/Night cycle

In this demo, we want to implement a basic day/night cycle. To do that, we will attach this script to the **Direct Light** object:

```
using UnityEngine;

public class DayNightCycle : MonoBehaviour
{
    public event System.EventHandler OnChanged;
    public float dayDuration = 10.0f;
    public bool isNight { get; private set; }
    private Color dayColor;
    private Light lightComponent;
    void Start()
    {
        lightComponent = GetComponent<Light>();
        dayColor = lightComponent.color;
    }
    void Update()
    {
  Color nightColor = Color.white * 0.1f;
        float lightIntensity = 0.5f +
                    Mathf.Sin(Time.time * 2.0f * Mathf.PI / dayDuration) /
2.0f;
        if (isNight != (lightIntensity < 0.3))
        {
            isNight = !isNight;
            if (OnChanged != null)
                OnChanged(this, System.EventArgs.Empty);
        }
        lightComponent.color = Color.Lerp(nightColor, dayColor,
lightIntensity);
    }
}
```

This is a common day/night cycle script. The way it works is quite intuitive. Let's have a look:

- At each `Update` step, we update the `lightIntensity` variable according to a sinusoidal wave.
- The variable cycles from 0 to 1 and, when the value is smaller than 0.3, we decide that it is nighttime.
- Finally, we update the light color according to the lightIntensity value, interpolating the day color and the night color.
- Note the `onChanged` event. This is an event that we call every time we switch from day to night and from night to day. We will use this event to create an `IsNight` node in the Behavior Tree.

Design the Enemy Behavior

Now, it is time to design the enemy, behavior. Before writing a single line of code, we need to design the enemy behavior:

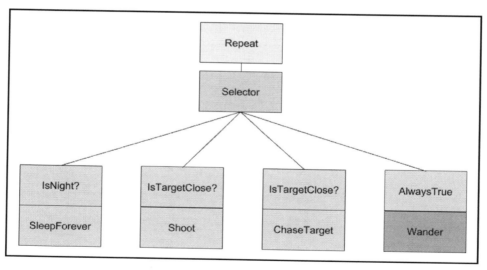

This is our draft. The tree describes the following behavior:

1. If it is night, the enemy is deactivated.
2. If the target is very close, then the enemy shoots at the target.
3. If the target is a bit further away, the enemy chases the target.
4. Otherwise, the enemy just wanders around.

There are two important things to note:

- First, the two `IsTargetClose` nodes differ in the value we consider *close*. In particular, we want to shoot the target only if we are really close to the target; otherwise, we just start chasing it.
- Second, and most important, the order of the nodes matters. Because the `Selector` works in order from left to right and stops at the first `Success`, we cannot put `ChaseTarget` before `Shoot`, otherwise the enemy will never `Shoot`!

As a rule of thumb, conditions are ordered from the most restrictive (that is, the one with the highest priority) to the most relaxed (and, in fact, we put `AlwaysTrue` at the very end).

Note also that `Wander` is in a different color. This is because it is not a node, but another Behavior Tree. In fact, a nice property of BTs is that you can use reuse common BTs as nodes inside more complex BTs. The `Wander` BT just makes our enemy move randomly on the map; fortunately, it is already included in Behavior Bricks, so we don't need to implement it!

Implement the Nodes

After we have made a plan for our Behavior Tree, the next step is to check whether our BT implementation of choice (in our case, Behavior Bricks) already includes some of the nodes. Of course, we want to reuse as much pre-made nodes as possible. Reading the Behaviors Bricks documentation, we can see that it already includes nodes such as `IsTargetClose`, `MoveToGameObject`, `Wander`, and `AlwaysTrue`, plus, of course, `Repeat` and `Selectors`.

Therefore, we need to write all the rest. Let's look at a step-by-step process to do this:

1. Let's start with `Shoot`. First, we create a simple Action called `ShootOnce` that just shoots a single bullet:

```
using Pada1.BBCore;
using Pada1.BBCore.Tasks;
using BBUnity.Actions;
```

```
[Action("Chapter09/ShootOnce")]
[Help("Clone a 'bullet' and shoots it through the Forward axis
with the " +
        "specified velocity.")]
class ShootOnce : GOAction {
  // ....
}
```

At the beginning, we import Behavior Bricks modules. Then, we create the ShootOnce class by extending the generic GOAction class.

Note the class attributes; they are used by Behavior Bricks to populate the BT visual editor. In the Action attribute, we specify that this Action is, indeed, an action, and can be found in the Chapter09 collection with the name ShootOnce. The Help attribute is just a basic description of this action's purpose.

2. We describe the class attributes as usual. The only difference is that we decorate each attribute with the InParam attribute, which specifies that the following value must be retrieved from the blackboard:

```
[InParam("shootPoint")]
public Transform shootPoint;

[InParam("bullet")]
public GameObject bullet;

[InParam("velocity", DefaultValue = 30f)]
public float velocity;
```

For this Action, we need a Bullet prefab, a place to instantiate the bullet (shootPoint) and the bullet velocity. Later, we will see how to set them up from the visual interface.

3. Now, it is time to write the real meat:

```
public override void OnStart()
{
    if (shootPoint == null)
    {
        shootPoint = gameObject.transform.Find("shootPoint");
        if (shootPoint == null)
        {
            Debug.LogWarning("Shoot point not specified. ShootOnce
will not work " +
                            "for " + gameObject.name);
        }
```

```
        }
        base.OnStart();
    }

    public override TaskStatus OnUpdate()
    {
        if (shootPoint == null)
        {
            return TaskStatus.FAILED;
        }
        GameObject newBullet = GameObject.Instantiate(
                            bullet, shootPoint.position,
                            shootPoint.rotation *
bullet.transform.rotation
                                ) as GameObject;
        // Give it a velocity
        if (newBullet.GetComponent<Rigidbody>() == null) {
            newBullet.AddComponent<Rigidbody>();
        }
        newBullet.GetComponent<Rigidbody>().velocity = velocity *
shootPoint.forward;
        return TaskStatus.COMPLETED;
    }
```

Every Behavior Bricks Node contains some default method called during the BT execution that can be overwritten in our custom implementations. In this example, we see two of them: OnStart and OnUpdate. They are used very similarly to how we use Start and Update in MonoBehavior:

- In OnStart, which is called when the BT is created, we just initialize all the references we need; in this case, we get a reference to the shootPoint object. Note also that we must call base.OnStart(); to initialize the base class.
- In OnUpdate, we write the intended action for the Node, that is, what we want this node to do when it is invoked. In this case, the code is self-explanatory: we create a bullet and we shoot it by setting a velocity.

If there is no problem, we mark the node as complete (so that the BT knows that it is a Success); otherwise (for example, if the shootPoint is not set), we mark the node as Failed.

4. Now that we have a base class for shooting once, we can create a new `Action` for shooting continuously:

```
[Action("Chapter09/Shoot")]
[Help("Periodically clones a 'bullet' and shoots it through the
Forward axis " +
      "with the specified velocity. This action never ends.")]
public class Shoot : ShootOnce
{

    [InParam("delay", DefaultValue = 30)]
    public int delay;

    // Game loops since the last shoot.
    private int elapsed = 0;

    public override TaskStatus OnUpdate()
    {
        if (delay > 0)
        {
            ++elapsed;
            elapsed %= delay;
            if (elapsed != 0)
                return TaskStatus.RUNNING;
        }

        base.OnUpdate();
        return TaskStatus.RUNNING;
    }
}
```

This class simply extends the `ShootOnce` class, adds a delay attribute (it is the time between consecutive shots), and then continuously reruns its parent class (`ShootOnce`). Note that this Action always returns `RUNNING`, meaning that this action never completes as long as the BT selects it.

5. In the same way, we can create the remaining `Action`. For instance, the `SleepForever` action is very straightforward: it just does nothing and suspends the execution of the BTs. Note that the class extends `BasePrimitiveAction`, which is the most basic form of `Action` in Behavior Bricks:

```
[Action("Chapter09/SleepForever")]
[Help("Low-cost infinite action that never ends. It does not
consume CPU at all.")]

public class SleepForever : BasePrimitiveAction
```

```
{
    public override TaskStatus OnUpdate()
    {
        return TaskStatus.SUSPENDED;
    }

}
```

6. Finally, we need to implement the `IsNight` condition. The code is shown in the following listing:

```
[Condition("Chapter09/IsNight")]
[Help("Checks whether it is night time.")]
public class IsNightCondition : ConditionBase
{

    private DayNightCycle light;

    public override bool Check()
    {
        if (searchLight())
        {
            return light.isNight;
        }
        else
        {
            return false;
        }
    }

    public override TaskStatus MonitorCompleteWhenTrue()
    {
        if (Check())
        {
            // Light is off. It's night right now.
            return TaskStatus.COMPLETED;
        }
        else
        {
            if (light != null)
            {
                light.OnChanged += OnSunset;
            }
            return TaskStatus.SUSPENDED;
            // We will never awake if light does not exist.
        }
    }
```

```csharp
    public override TaskStatus MonitorFailWhenFalse()
    {
        if (!Check())
        {
            // Light does not exist, or is "on" (daylight).
Condition is false.
            return TaskStatus.FAILED;
        }
        else
        {
            // Light exists, and is "off" (night). We suspend
ourselves
            // until sunrise (when the condition will become
false).
            light.OnChanged += OnSunrise;
            return TaskStatus.SUSPENDED;
        }
    }

    public void OnSunset(object sender, System.EventArgs night)
    {
        light.OnChanged -= OnSunset;
        EndMonitorWithSuccess();
    }

    public void OnSunrise(object sender, System.EventArgs e)
    {
        light.OnChanged -= OnSunrise;
        EndMonitorWithFailure();
    }

    public override void OnAbort()
    {
        if (searchLight())
        {
            light.OnChanged -= OnSunrise;
            light.OnChanged -= OnSunset;
        }
        base.OnAbort();
    }

    // Search the global light, and stores in the light field. It
returns true
    // if the light was found.
    private bool searchLight()
    {
        if (light != null)
        {
```

```
            return true;
        }

        GameObject lightGO =
GameObject.FindGameObjectWithTag("MainLight");
        if (lightGO == null)
        {
            return false;
        }

        light = lightGO.GetComponent<DayNightCycle>();
        return light != null;
    } // searchLight

}
```

This class is more complex, so let's go slow. First of all, `IsNight` extends `ConditionBase`, which is a basic condition template in Behavior Bricks. This class does a simple job: when it starts, it searches for a light with the `MainLight` tag. If that exists, it takes its `DayNightCycle` reference, stores it in the `light` variable, and registers with the `OnChanged` event. Then, every time we ask for this condition, we check whether the `isNight` variable in `light` is true or false (see the `Check` method).

However, checking this every time would be very inefficient, in general. So, the `BaseCondition` class contains two helpful functions:

- `MonitorCompleteWhenTrue` is a function that is called by the BT executor when the last returned value is false and, in practice, sets up a system that suspends BT execution until the variable became true again
- `MonitorFailWhenFalse`, is a dual function: it is called when the monitored value is true and suspends BT execution until the variable switches to false

For instance, let's look at `MonitorCompleteWhenTrue`. If `Check` is true (so it is night), we simply return `Complete`; otherwise, we register the `OnSunset` function with the `OnChanged` event. When the day/night cycle switch from day to night, `OnSunset` is called and, in turn, `EndMonitorWithSuccess()` is called. `MonitorFailWhenFalse` works in the same way, but in the opposite direction (monitoring when we pass from night to day).

Building the Tree

Now that we have our nodes, we need to assemble the tree. To do that, follows these steps:

1. Right-click in the inspector and go to the **Create** sub-menu.
2. Then, select **Behavior Tree**.
3. Choose a location and save.
4. An empty editor window should show up onscreen; this is the tree editor.
5. You can right-click anywhere and start adding and connecting nodes.
6. To implement our tree, you need to recreate the tree shown in the following diagram:

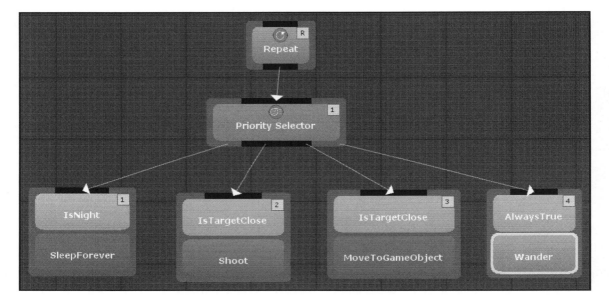

7. Select all the nodes, one at a time, and look for the input parameters; these are the parameters we specified in our classes. These parameters may be **CONSTANT**, meaning that we directly write a value for them, or a **BLACKBOARD** reference.
8. We need to set up the parameters with the following values:
    - In the first `IsTargerClose`, we specify the blackboard `player` as **target** and the constant 7 as **closeDistance** (if the player is not listed, click on **New Parameter**)
    - In the second `IsTargerClose`, we specify the blackboard `player` as **target** and the constant 20 as **closeDistance**

- In `Shoot`, we need to set 30 as the delay, the blackboard `shootPoint` as **shootPoint** (you probably need to create it with **New Parameter**), the blackboard `bullet` as the **bullet** prefab (create it if missing), and the constant 30 as **velocity**
- In `MoveToGameObject`, the **target** is the `player` value in the blackboard
- In `Wander`, we set a new blackboard parameter (`floor`) as **wanderArea**

Attach the BT to the Enemy

Now, it is time to attach this behavior tree to the Enemy's BT executor. For that, follow these steps:

1. Select the `Enemy` game object and add the **Behavior Executor** component to it.
2. In the **Behavior** field, drag and drop the behavior tree we created before.
3. In **Behavior Parameters**, a list of all the blackboard parameters we defined in the previous step (**player**, **floor**, **shootPoint**, and **bullet**) should appear.
4. Fill them with the appropriate objects, as shown in the following screenshot:

5. At this point, the enemy should be ready to go. Click play and you should see the enemy wandering around and, when close enough to the player, start chasing and shooting at it.

For more details, look at the code included in this book.

Summary

In this chapter, we explored the general background behind any behavior tree implementation. We have seen what a BT is, what their basic components are, and how can we use a BT to describe game character behavior. Then, we implemented a demo using a free plugin called Behavior Bricks. In the demo, we created the behavior for a simple scenario: the player and a patrolling robot. We also implemented a day/night cycle to spice up the scenario.

Behavior Trees are the cornerstones of modern AI for game characters. Implementation details and deeper examples would require a full book to explain fully. Luckily, the web is full of resources for the curious reader.

External Resources

- The official Behavior Bricks project page from the Complutense University of Madrid in Spain http://gaia.fdi.ucm.es/research/bb/
- Behavior Bricks official documentation: http://bb.padaonegames.com/doku.php
- Chris Simpson (the developer of Project Zomboid) wrote a nice explanation of BTs on Gamasutra: https://www.gamasutra.com/blogs/ChrisSimpson/20140717/221339/Behavior_trees_for_AI_How_they_work.php.
- Chapter 6 of GameAI Pro, which explores many implementation details of BTs (in C++), is free and available at the following link: https://www.gameaipro.com/GameAIPro/GameAIPro_Chapter06_The_Behavior_Tree_Starter_Kit.pdf.

Machine Learning in Unity **10**

Machine learning is the hottest buzzword in **artificial intelligence (AI)**. Nowadays, everything contains (or claims to contain) some machine learning-powered AI that is supposed to improve our life: calendars, to-do apps, photo management software, every smartphone, and much more. Even if most of the times, the use of the phrase "machine learning" is just a marketing gimmick, it is indisputable that machine learning has improved significantly in recent years and, most importantly, there are tools that allow everybody to implement a learning algorithm without any previous AI knowledge.

So what about video games? We sure want to avoid missing the machine-learning train, don't we? Fortunately, Unity provides a complete toolkit for machine learning that spares us the complication of interfacing the game engine with an external machine-learning framework.

In this chapter, we will look at the following topics:

- An introduction to the Unity Machine Learning Agents Toolkit
- Set up the Unity Machine Learning Agents Toolkit
- See how to run a simple example

Machine learning is an extensive topic, therefore, we do not expect to cover every single aspect of it. For further reference, look at the toolkit documentation and in the additional resources linked at the end of this chapter.

The Unity Machine Learning Agents Toolkit

The Unity Machine Learning Agents Toolkit (*ML-Agents Toolkit* for short) is a collection of software and plugins that help writing autonomous game agents powered by machine learning algorithms. You can explore and download the source code at the GitHub repository at `https://github.com/Unity-Technologies/ml-agents`.

The ML-Agents Toolkit is based on the reinforcement learning algorithm. In a very simplistic way, reinforcement learning is the algorithmic equivalent of training a dog. If you want to teach a dog some trick, you give him a command and then, when the dog does what you expect, you give him a reward. The reward tells your dog that it is responding correctly to a command and, therefore, the next time it hears the same command, it will do the same thing to get a new reward:

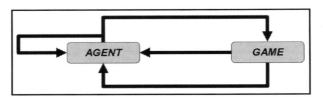

 In reinforcement learning, you can also punish your agent when it does the wrong things, but in the dog-training example, I can assure you that a punishment is completely unnecessary. Just give him rewards!

For an AI agent trained with reinforcement learning, we perform a similar cycle:

1. When an agent performs an action, the action will influence the world (as in, change the agent position, move an object around, collect a coin, gain score points, and so on).
2. The algorithm then sends back to the agent the new world state with a reward (or punishment).
3. When the agent needs to decide its next action, it will choose the action that maximizes the expected reward (or minimizes the expected punishment).

For this reason, it is clear that training a reinforcement learning agent requires several simulations of the scenario in which the agent performs an action, receives a reward, updates its decision making values, performs another action, and so on. This work is offloaded from Unity to TensorFlow, Google's popular library for machine learning and neural network training.

For more information on reinforcement learning, look at the additional resources at the end of the chapter. Let's now see how to install the toolkit.

How to install the ML-Agents Toolkit

As a first step, we need to download the toolkit. We can do this by cloning the repository with the following command:

```
git clone https://github.com/Unity-Technologies/ml-agents.git
```

This creates an ml-agents folder in your current position. The ML-Agents Toolkit is composed of three main components:

- A Unity plugin (stored in the UnitySDK subfolder).
- A Python package containing the Python interface for Unity and for TensorFlow's trainers (stored in the ml-agents folder)
- A Python package containing the interface with OpenAI Gym (https://gym. openai.com/), a toolkit for training reinforcement learning agents (stored in the gym-unity folder).

 Git is the most famous version-control application in the world. It is used to store your source code, keep track of different versions, collaborate with other people, and much more. If you are not already using Git, you should really check it out. You can download it from https://git-scm. com/.

Now it is time to install the required dependencies. As we have said before, the ML-Agents Toolkit requires Python and TensorFlow to work properly. Don't worry, you do not need to know the Python language to use these (although it may help).

Installing Python and TensorFlow on Windows

The fastest way to install Python and TensorFlow in Windows is by using the Anaconda distribution (https://www.anaconda.com/).

 Anaconda comes by default with the latest version of Python (3.7 at the time of this writing), which is not compatible with the ML-Toolkit. Don't worry—after you install Anaconda, you can force Python 3.6 with the conda install python=3.6 command.

1. Go on the Anaconda's website and download Anaconda.
2. After the installation, open the Anaconda Prompt command line and type:

```
conda create -n ml-agents python=3.6
```

With this command, we create an Anaconda environment for the ML-Agents Toolkit. We call this new environment ml-agents and we will use Python 3.6.

3. If you get a message like "**conda is not recognized as internal or external command**", this means that you don't have the right environment variables for Anaconda. In such a case, do the following:
    1. Go to your environment variable editor by typing `edit environment variables` in the Windows menu and then clicking on **Environment Variables**.
    2. Add the following values to the `Path` variable:

        ```
        %UserProfile%\Anaconda3\Scripts
        %UserProfile%\Anaconda3
        ```

4. Activate the new environment with `activate ml-agents`. You should see `(ml-agents)` on the left of your prompt.
5. Finally, let's install TensorFlow in the environment:

    ```
    pip install tensorflow==1.7.1
    ```

6. Return to the folder in which we cloned the ML-Agents Toolkit.
7. Go in the ml-agents subfolder and install all the dependencies with the following command:

    ```
    pip install .
    ```

8. If everything is successful, you should be able to run the `mlagents-learn --help` command without any problems.

Installing Python and TensorFlow on macOS and Unix-like systems

To install the ML-Agents Toolkit on macOS or Linux, you need first to install Python 3.6 (at the moment, the ML-Agents Toolkit works only with Python 3.6).

Then, just go in the `ml-agents` subfolder and run the following command:

```
pip3 install .
```

If everything is correct, you should be able to run the `mlagents-learn --help` command without any errors.

 Pip3 is automatically installed with any Python 3.x distribution. If, for some reason, you don't have pip3 installed, try following the official guide: `https://pip.pypa.io/en/latest/installing/`

Using the ML-Agents Toolkit – a basic example

Now that the everything is installed, we can start using the ML-Agents Toolkit. First, let's explain the three main entities in the toolkit:

- The Agent: Obviously, the agent is the central object in the ML-Agents Toolkit. An agent is an object that performs an action, receives information from the environment, and can receive rewards for actions.
- The Brain object: The Brain object is responsible for choosing the agent's actions. At the moment, there are four different Brain types:
  - Player mode: The agent executes actions decided by player input.
  - Heuristic mode: The agent executes actions decided by some hard-coded decision-making system (for example, a Behavior Tree).
  - External mode: The agent executes actions decided by TensorFlow. The brain will communicate with it using the Python API interface.
  - Internal mode: This is a very experimental Brain object, which we won't discuss in this book. However, what we can say is that this Brain object takes decisions using an embedded version of TensorFlow written in C# (called *TensorFlowSharp* or *TFSharp*).
- The Academy: This stores the training configurations, the scenario parameters, and a list of all the Brains in the scene.

To start using the ML- Agents toolkit, we need to do the following:

1. Open Unity and create an empty project.
2. Navigate through your hard drive until you locate the UnitySDK folder in the repository we cloned before, and copy the **ML-Agents** folder from `UnitySDK/Assets` into our project:

3. We need to make sure that we are using the right runtime. To do this, go to **Edit | Project Settings | Player** and, for each platform (PC, Mac, Android, and so on), go into **Other Settings** and make sure that the **Scripting Runtime Version** is set to **.NET 4.x Equivalent**, and that in **Scripting Define Symbols*** there is the **ENABLE_TENSORFLOW** value. If not, adjust these settings to be as we need them, and then save, as follows:

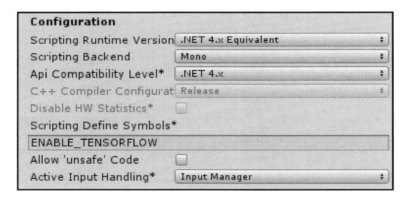

Creating the scene

Let's follow a step-by-step procedure to create our scene:

1. Create a simple 3D scene with a lane, a sphere, and a cube, as shown in the following screenshot:

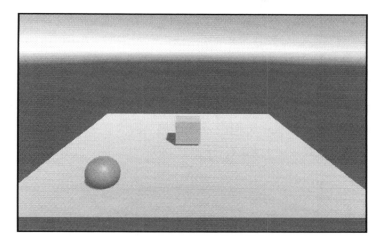

2. Add a Rigidbody component to the sphere.
3. Now we need to create the Academy—let's create an empty object and call it Academy.
4. Then we create another empty object inside Academy, and call it Brain.

Implementing the code

Now we need to implement the code that will describe the agent's behavior and the ML-Agent's Academy. The agent's behavior script describes the way the agents performs actions in the simulation, the reward it receives, and the way we reset it to start a new simulation:

1. Click on the Academy and add to it a new script called SphereAcademy with the following code:

```
using MLAgents;
public class SphereAcademy : Academy { }
```

This will create a default training academy for our agent.

2. Select the Brain object and add the Brain script to it.

3. Select the Sphere. Let's add to it a new script, called SphereAgent, with the following contents:

```
using System.Collections.Generic;
using UnityEngine;
using MLAgents;

public class SphereAgent : Agent
{
  Rigidbody rBody;
  void Start () {
  rBody = GetComponent<Rigidbody>();
}

public Transform Target;

public override void AgentReset()
{
  if (this.transform.position.y < -1.0)
  {
    // The agent fell
    this.transform.position = Vector3.zero;
    this.rBody.angularVelocity = Vector3.zero;
    this.rBody.velocity = Vector3.zero;
  }
  else
  {
   // Move the target to a new spot
   Target.position = new Vector3(Random.value * 8 - 4,
                     0.5f,
                     Random.value * 8 - 4);
  }
 }
}
```

This is the base agent for our demo. AgentReset() is a function called by the system every time we want to reset the training scene. In our example, we check if the sphere fell from the plane and we bring it back to zero; otherwise, we move it in a random location.

4. We need to add the CollectObservations method to the SphereAgent. This method is used by the agent to get information from the game world and then use it to perform a decision:

```
public override void CollectObservations()
{
```

```
// Calculate relative position
Vector3 relativePosition = Target.position -
this.transform.position;
// Relative position
AddVectorObs(relativePosition.x/5);
AddVectorObs(relativePosition.z/5);
// Distance to edges of platform
AddVectorObs((this.transform.position.x + 5)/5);
AddVectorObs((this.transform.position.x - 5)/5);
AddVectorObs((this.transform.position.z + 5)/5);
AddVectorObs((this.transform.position.z - 5)/5);
// agent velocity
AddVectorObs(rBody.velocity.x/5);
AddVectorObs(rBody.velocity.z/5);
}
```

In this example, we are interested in the following:

5. The relative position of the sphere agent from the cube (the target). We are only interested in the X and Z values, because the sphere only moves on the plane (note that we normalize the values dividing by 5: that is half the default plane size).

   - The distance from the plane edges.
   - The sphere's velocity.

6. We need to implement the AgentAction method. This method is called whenever the agent needs to perform an action. The method takes two parameters:
   - vectorAction, containing abstract inputs from the system (the size and type of the vector is specified in the agent's brain setting)
   - textAction, a string specifying the input action name (in case the action is a discrete value instead of a numeric input)

In our case, the actions are numeric and correspond to the force strength values in the X and Z directions.

The AgentAction method will also provide rewards for the agent (if we reach the cube) or punishment (if we fall off the plane).

7. The final version of the code is the following:

```
private float speed = 10;
private float previousDistance = float.MaxValue;

public override void AgentAction(float[] vectorAction, string
textAction)
{
  // Rewards
  float distanceToTarget =
Vector3.Distance(this.transform.position,
  Target.position);

  // Reached target
  if (distanceToTarget < 1.42f)
  {
    AddReward(1.0f);
    Done();
  }

  // Time penalty
  AddReward(-0.05f);

  // Fell off platform
  if (this.transform.position.y < -1.0)
  {
    AddReward(-1.0f);
    Done();
  }

  // Actions, size = 2
  Vector3 controlSignal = Vector3.zero;
  controlSignal.x = vectorAction[0];
  controlSignal.z = vectorAction[1];
  rBody.AddForce(controlSignal * speed);
}
```

As you can see, we add a 0.05 penalty for each frame we consume to reach the goal, a -1 penalty if we fall off, and a +1 reward if we reach the cube. The Done() function is used to signal that we reached the end of the simulation and, therefore, we need a reset.

Adding the final touches

Now we need to connect all the pieces together in to make the demo work. We to attach the `SphereAgent` script to the sphere, the `SphereAcademy` script to the `Academy` object and, of course, attach the `Brain` to the agent:

1. We need to connect the `Brain` object to the `SphereAgent` component, as shown in the following screenshot:

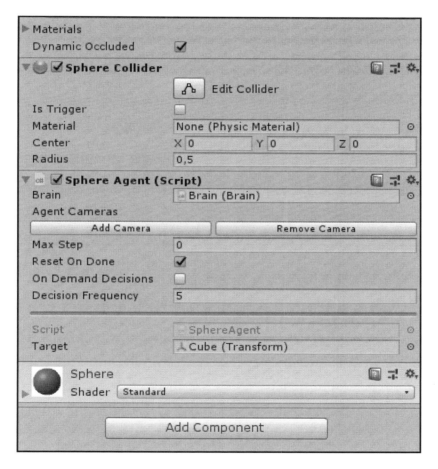

2. Set **Decision Frequency** to 5 and drag the cube object into the **Target** field.

Training a Brain object

Looking at pre-trained brains may be cool, but we really want is to train the brain ourselves! To do that, let's select one of the brains of our example. In the inspector, search for the Brain Type field and set it to External.

Now we need to configure the Brain as follows:

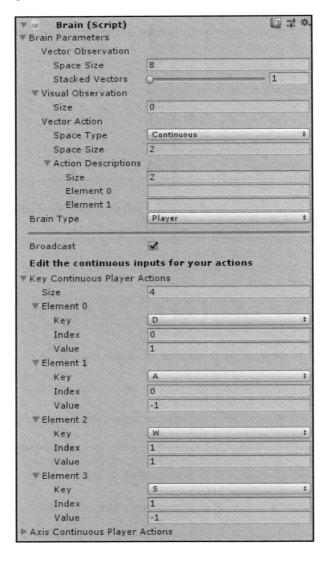

Now you can press Play and, because we set the Brain Type to Player, we should be able to move your sphere using the *WASD* keys. However, we want to use machine learning—so let's see how to train this agent!

Training the agent

The first step is to change the Brain Type from Player to External. Now, open a command-line interface and navigate to the ML-Agents Toolkit repository. Then run this command:

```
mlagents-learn config/trainer_config.yaml --run-id=firstRun --train
```

You should see something like this:

At this point, you can press the **Play** button on the Unity Editor and the training will begin.

After the training is complete (or after you press *Ctrl + C* to stop it), you should find the trained model at the `models/<run-identifier>/editor_<academy_name>_<run-identifier>.bytes` path, where `<academy_name>` is the name of the Academy object in the demo.

If you want to run the demo with the trained model, go to the Brain, switch Brain Type to Internal and drag this file to the Graph Model placeholder. Then press Play and you should be able to see the sphere moving to the cubic target. Note that we write no code for this behavior: the agent learned the behavior by itself.

 If you get an error when you switch to the internal Brain, then you probably need to install the TFSharp plugin. You can download it from here: `https://s3.amazonaws.com/unity-ml-agents/0.5/TFSharpPlugin.unitypackage`

Summary

In this chapter, we barely scratched the surface of machine learning and how to use machine learning for training Unity agents. We learned how to install Unity's official ML-Agents Toolkit; how to set up Academy, Brain, and Agents; and how to train the model. However, this is just a basic introduction to the ML-Agents Toolkit; there a lot of unexplored directions that are waiting for you.

With this chapter, we have covered all the basic gameplay AI techniques. In the next chapter, we will wrap everything up by developing an AI agent into a more complex game demo.

Further reading

- For more information, I encourage you to check the in-depth documentation for ML-Agents in the official repository (`https://github.com/Unity-Technologies/ml-agents/tree/master/docs`).
- For a more in-depth (but still very accessible) introduction to Reinforcement Learning there is a good article on freeCodeCamp (`https://medium.freecodecamp.org/an-introduction-to-reinforcement-learning-4339519de419`)

11
Putting It All Together

Over the previous nine chapters, we've looked at various AI techniques and built some simple demo applications using Unity3D. This is the final chapter in our book, in which we'll apply some of those techniques to a more complex game example. The techniques we'll be using in this chapter include navigation meshes and **finite-state machines (FSMs)**, but, more importantly, we will learn how to navigate and add AI into a pre-existing complex game. So, unlike the other chapters, this is a much more of a real-world scenario.

In this chapter, we'll add AI to a simple tank combat game. The game we'll start with is based on the *TANKS!* official Unity tutorial, which was in turn inspired by a historic tank game called *Combat* for the Atari 2600. In its default version, this is a straightforward multiplayer game. Each player takes control of a tank and the goal is to destroy each other. To make things more complicated, the player can decide the strength (and, thus, the distance) of the shot by pressing and holding the spacebar for a shorter or longer duration.

Because we are AI developers, we want to build an AI for the enemy tank so that we can play with ourselves. This is what we'll do in this chapter.

In this chapter, we will cover the following topics:

- Basic game structure
- Adding automated navigation
- Creating decision-making AI with FSM

Basic game structure

As we have said before, the game is based on the official Unity tutorial, *TANKS!* When we download the project, we are welcomed by a pleasant desert scenario, with rocks, structures, palm trees, and so on. The basic structure of the game is shown in the following screenshot:

 It may be helpful to follow the full Unity tutorial, available at `https://unity3d.com/learn/tutorials/s/tanks-tutorial`. It does not involve AI, but it will teach you a lot of other important stuff for game development, such as how to design a game manager, basic controls, audio, and so on.

The first time you start with an existing project, spend as much time as you can familiarizing yourself with the game structure, the basic scripts, and the components. It is important that you can operate at ease in a project that you don't know. To do this, run the game a couple of times, try small modifications to the code to see the effect, and add Debug messages to learn about the flow in which information moves around the game. The following image will give you an idea on how the game will look when we run it:

Adding automated navigation

The first step is to modify the level to support automated navigation. In the original game, all the moving objects (the tanks) are controlled by the user, so there is no need for pathfinding. Now that we want to add AI, we need to have a world representation through which the AI can move. Luckily, this process is very easy, thanks to NavMeshes.

Creating the NavMesh

To do this, implement the following:

1. Open the Navigation windows (**Window** I **AI** I **Navigation**) and look at the NavMesh generation parameters.

   In this case, NavMesh generation is quite easy: we are only interested in moving around on the ground surface plane, so there are no jumps, no links, and no slopes we need to care of.

2. The only adjustment to the default NavMesh parameters we need to make is for the baking agent size (that is, the sizes of the virtual agent used by Unity to verify if a location is large enough to allow the agent to pass).

3. In fact, the tanks used in the game are about 3 units large, so we need to instruct the generator to remove the areas that are too small for the tank to pass through:

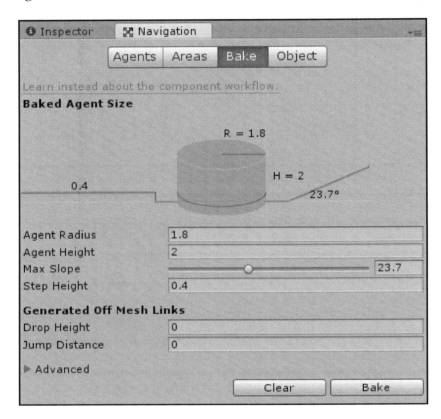

In the preceding screenshot, just to be safe, we use an **Agent Radius** of 1.8, and reduce the **Max Slope** value to about 20 (after all, we are not interested in slopes: the game is completely flat).

4. After that, press **Bake**. You should get a nice NavMesh, as in the following screenshot:

5. We now want to add some patrolling points that the AI tank can follow. To do this, we create an empty GameObject; feel free to create as many other GameObject instances as you like.

6. Then, we create a tag, `PatrolPoint`, and tag all the patrol points with it:

Now that we have a world representation and a set of points that we can use to wander around, we need to create an agent controlled by the AI.

Setting up the agent

Unfortunately, the game does not support AI, so we need to add the agent by ourselves. To do this, use the following steps:

1. We have to identify the player tank. As you can see from the game hierarchy, there is no tank in the scene. In fact, as you should know from your preliminary exploration, the tanks are spawned by the `GameManager`. The tank model we'll use is actually a prefab called `CompleteTank`.
2. Let's copy the prefab and call it CompleteTankAI.
3. Then we need to add the **Nav Mesh Agent** component to it. This allows the tank to move around on our new NavMesh:

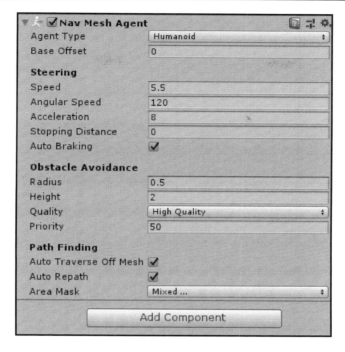

But this is not enough. First, we'll reuse the TankShooting script from the *TANKS!* demo, so we need to disable shooting if this script is attached to an AI (otherwise, the player could shoot for the AI agent).

4. For this, we create a public Boolean variable, called m_IsAI, and add the following lines to the Update script:

```
private void Update ()
    {
        if (m_IsAI)
        {
            return;
        }
    ...
```

These lines just stop the Update script for the AI agent, thereby disabling player input for AI characters. We also need to add another *patch*; in fact, if we disable input, we will disable also the shoot *strength*.

5. So, we need to add this back into the Fire function:

```
public void Fire ()
    {
```

```
                        // Set the fired flag so only Fire is only called once.
                        m_Fired = true;

                        // Create an instance of the shell and store a
            reference to it's rigidbody.
                        Rigidbody shellInstance =
                            Instantiate (m_Shell, m_FireTransform.position,
            m_FireTransform.rotation) as Rigidbody;

                        // If AI, we shoot with average force.
                        if (m_IsAI)
                        {
                            m_CurrentLaunchForce = m_MaxLaunchForce / 2.0f;
                        }
                        // Set the shell's velocity to the launch force in the
            fire position's forward direction.
                        shellInstance.velocity = m_CurrentLaunchForce *
            m_FireTransform.forward;

                        // Change the clip to the firing clip and play it.
                        m_ShootingAudio.clip = m_FireClip;
                        m_ShootingAudio.Play ();

                        // Reset the launch force.  This is a precaution in
            case of missing button events.
                        m_CurrentLaunchForce = m_MinLaunchForce;
                    }
```

For simplicity, we are replacing the variable shooting force with a constant shooting force.

As an exercise, you could try to make `m_CurrentLaunchForce` a parameter of the `Fire()` functions. Note also that we make the `Fire()` function public: in fact, we need to call this function from the FSM that we'll implement later.

6. Then, we need to do something similar to the Tank Movement script. We add an `m_IsAI` variable and, if true, we disable player input:

```
void Update ()
    {
        if (!m_IsAI)
        {
            // Store the value of both input axes.
            m_MovementInputValue =
            Input.GetAxis(m_MovementAxisName);
            m_TurnInputValue = Input.GetAxis(m_TurnAxisName);
```

```
    }

        EngineAudio ();
    }
```

Another change to the AI tank is to delete the Tank Movement component from the prefab. Instead, we will use FSM and pathfinding to move the tank, as we will see in the following sections.

Fixing the GameManager script

As a final step, we need to instruct the GameManager script to spawn a player tank and an AI tank.

1. Open the GameManager script and add a new public variable in which we'll store the new AI tank prefab:

```
        public GameObject m_TankPrefab;              // Reference to
    the prefab the players will control.
            public GameObject m_TankAIPrefab;          // Reference to
    the prefab the AI will control.
```

2. Then modify the SpawnAll function in this way:

```
        private void SpawnAllTanks()
        {
            // For all the tanks...
            for (int i = 0; i < m_Tanks.Length; i++)
            {
                if (i == m_Tanks.Length - 1)
                {
                    // If last tank, it's AI
                    m_Tanks[i].m_Instance =
                        Instantiate(m_TankAIPrefab,
    m_Tanks[i].m_SpawnPoint.position, m_Tanks[i].m_SpawnPoint.rotation)
    as GameObject;
                    m_Tanks[i].m_PlayerNumber = i + 1;
                    m_Tanks[i].Setup();
                }
                else
                {
                    // ... create them, set their player number and
    references needed for control.
                    m_Tanks[i].m_Instance =
                        Instantiate(m_TankPrefab,
    m_Tanks[i].m_SpawnPoint.position, m_Tanks[i].m_SpawnPoint.rotation)
```

```
            as GameObject;
                                m_Tanks[i].m_PlayerNumber = i + 1;
                                m_Tanks[i].Setup();
                    }

            }
        }
```

This is not very elegant, but it works. We just check if we are spawning the last tank and, if we are, we spawn the `m_TankAIPrefab` model.

3. Finally, just add the prefab to the inspector as follows:

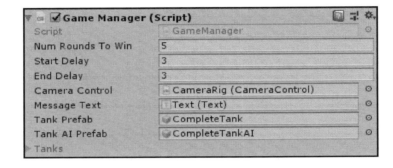

Creating decision-making AI with FSM

In `Chapter 2`, *Finite State Machines*, we saw how to implement a simple FSM. In this section, we are using the same technique, but will apply it to the more complex scenario of this demo.

First of all, we need an FSM plan. For this demo, we are interested only in how to connect the FSM to the existing game, so we will keep it simple. The FSM for our tank is composed of just two states, patrolling and shooting.

The plan is nice and simple:

- The AI tank starts in the Patrol state, and wanders around the patrolling points we defined before.
- Then, if the players get in range, the tank switches into the Attack state.
- In the Attack state, the tank turns toward the player and start shooting at it.
- Finally, if we are in the Attack state and the players leaves the AI's range, the tank will go back to the Patrol state.

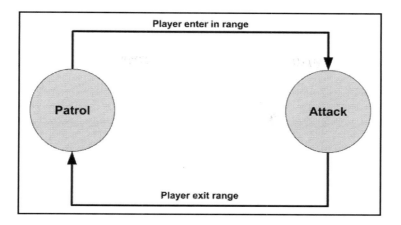

For the implementation, do the following:

1. Let's start with the FSM class:

```
using UnityEngine;
using System.Collections;

public class FSM : Complete.TankMovement
{
    //Next destination position of the NPC Tank
    protected Vector3 destPos;

    //List of points for patrolling
    protected GameObject[] pointList;

    protected virtual void Initialize() { }
    protected virtual void FSMUpdate() { }
    protected virtual void FSMFixedUpdate() { }

    // Use this for initialization
    void Start()
    {
        Initialize();
    }

    // Update is called once per frame
    void Update()
    {
        FSMUpdate();
    }

    void FixedUpdate()
```

```
    {
        FSMFixedUpdate();
    }
}
```

As you can see, this class extends the `Complete.TankMovement`. In this way, we can reuse the existing `TankMovement` code for things like the engine sounds and other cosmetic aspects.

As explained in `Chapter 2`, *Finite State Machines*, the FSM class stores the fundamental data we need for our decision-making AI, plus functions that can be overwritten by the actual Tank Controller for the `Update`, `FixedUpdate`, and `Start` methods (the default functions, in fact, cannot be overwritten directly). In the `FSM` class, we want to store all the patrol points and the destination point (that is, the current patrol point the tank is looking for).

2. Now, it is time for the full controller. We create a new `AITankControler` script with the following initial content:

```
using UnityEngine;
using System;
using UnityEngine.AI;

public class AITankController : FSM
{
    public Complete.TankShooting tankShooter;
    public Complete.TankHealth tankHealth;

    private bool isDead = false;
    private float elapsedTime = 0.0f;
    private float shootRate = 3.0f;

    private GameObject player = null;
    private NavMeshAgent navMeshAgent;

    public enum FSMState
    {
        None,
        Patrol,
        Attack,
        Dead,
    }

    //Current state that the NPC is reaching
    public FSMState curState;
    ...
```

In the preceding code, the class starts by extending F SM, of course, and defining the states. As you can see in the FSMState enum, we have Patrol and Attack, but also an empty state (None) and a final state (Dead). Then we add some class attributes to store the data we need.

The first two attributes are references to the TankShooter and TankHealth scripts in the tank. We will use them to check health and to fire bullets. Then we have an isDead Boolean to stop the FSM execution. Then we have elapsedTime and shootRate for controlling how rapidly the tank will shoot. Then, we have two private attributes that store a reference to the player (if in range) and a reference to NavMeshAgent. Lastly, we have a variable storing the current state in the FSM.

3. The Initialize function is used to initialize, of course, the FSM:

```
//Initialize the Finite state machine for the NPC tank
protected override void Initialize()
{

    navMeshAgent = GetComponent<NavMeshAgent>();

    //Get the list of points
    pointList =
GameObject.FindGameObjectsWithTag("PatrolPoint");

    int rndIndex = UnityEngine.Random.Range(0,
pointList.Length);
    destPos = pointList[rndIndex].transform.position;

}
```

In this function, we do three things:

*   We get the reference to the NavMeshAgent
*   We get the list of all the PatrolPoint in the scene
*   We randomly select one of the patrol points as the agent's current destination

4. Then it is time for the Update function, FSMUpdate:

```
protected override void FSMUpdate()
{
    switch (curState)
    {
        case FSMState.Patrol: UpdatePatrolState(); break;
        case FSMState.Attack: UpdateAttackState(); break;
```

```
            case FSMState.Dead: UpdateDeadState(); break;
      }

      elapsedTime += Time.deltaTime;

      //Go to dead state is no health left
      if (this.tankHealth.m_CurrentHealth <= 0)
          curState = FSMState.Dead;
   }
```

As we explained before, the main task for the Update function is to invoke the right function depending on the current state. In addition to that, FSMUpdate also updates the elapsedTime timer and sets the agent to the Dead state if the tank has no health.

5. The Dead state is very simple: the tank does nothing, and writes on the console that it is dead:

```
   private void UpdateDeadState()
      {
          if (!isDead)
          {
              Debug.Log("Dead");
          }
      }
```

6. The Attack state is more interesting:

```
   private void UpdateAttackState()
      {

          Collider[] players =
   Physics.OverlapSphere(transform.position, 15.0f,
   LayerMask.GetMask("Players"));
          if (players.Length == 0)
          {
              curState = FSMState.Patrol;
              player = null;
              navMeshAgent.enabled = true;
              return;
          }

          player = players[0].gameObject;

          Vector3 _direction = (player.transform.position -
   transform.position).normalized;
          Quaternion _lookRotation =
```

```
Quaternion.LookRotation(_direction);
        transform.rotation = Quaternion.Slerp(transform.rotation,
_lookRotation, Time.deltaTime * 3);

        if (elapsedTime > shootRate)
        {
            this.tankShooter.Fire();
            elapsedTime = 0;
        }
    }
```

In the first part of the preceding code, we cast a sphere using Unity's physics engine in order to "see" all the "Players" in a radius of 15 units. Then, if there is none (meaning that the player is out of range), we switch to the `Patrol` state, remove the player reference, enable the `NavMeshAgent` component, and terminate the state. Otherwise, we proceed with the attack: we get the player reference, we rotate the tank in its direction and we shoot (at the right rate). Luckily, the `Fire` function was already implemented in the original game! That's why good class design is important: if a class is functional, you can reutilize it very well, even for things that you didn't originally consider!

7. Finally, we have the `Patrol` state function:

```
private void UpdatePatrolState()
{
    Collider[] players =
Physics.OverlapSphere(transform.position, 10.0f,
LayerMask.GetMask("Players"));

    if (players.Length > 0)
    {
        curState = FSMState.Attack;
        player = players[0].gameObject;
        navMeshAgent.enabled = false;
        return;
    }

    if (IsInCurrentRange(destPos))
    {
        int rndIndex = UnityEngine.Random.Range(0,
pointList.Length);
        destPos = pointList[rndIndex].transform.position;
    }

    navMeshAgent.destination = destPos;
}
```

If no player is in range, then we proceed to wander around. First, we check if we have reached the current destination. If so, we need to select a new destination. Then, we set up the patrol point as the destination of the navMeshAgent component (as described in Chapter 8, *Navigation Meshes*).

8. The IsInCurrentRange function is just a simple comparison, as shown in the following code:

```
protected bool IsInCurrentRange(Vector3 pos)
{
    float xPos = Mathf.Abs(pos.x - transform.position.x);
    float zPos = Mathf.Abs(pos.z - transform.position.z);

    if (xPos <= 5 && zPos <= 5)
        return true;

    return false;
}
```

9. That's it. Add the AITankController script to the AITank prefab and connect all the required elements. You can see how the AITankController script should look in the following screenshot:

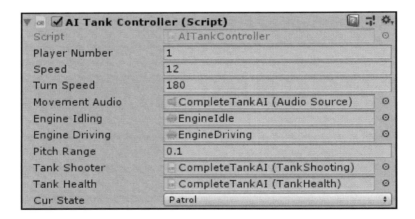

10. At this point, everything should be in place. Run the game and enjoy your simple tank moving around, shooting at you.

Summary

In this chapter, we applied some of the AI techniques that we learned previously to our simple tanks combat game. We'd be able to apply some more techniques in a larger game scope, but in this short chapter, we reused the simple FSM framework that we built in Chapter 2, *Finite State Machines*, as well as Unity's built-in navigation meshes capabilities.

This example project is a very good starting point for exploring the AI techniques that we introduced in this book. There are many improvements that can be implemented, and I really encourage you to play a bit more with this demo, trying to improve the AI. There are several low-hanging fruit, so, here are my suggestions:

As a first exercise, you can increase the number of states, for instance, by adding a Chasing state in which the tank will actively look for the player. The structure is similar to the Attack state, but with a bigger radius. As a bigger step, try to replace the FSM with a Behavior tree. The Behavior Tree that we implemented in the Behavior Tree demo is incredibly fitting in this scenario. Of course, you need to change the script in order to call the right function for the tank game, but it is a nice exercise.

We hope that you learned something new in areas related to artificial intelligence in games, as well as in Unity3D. We just scratched the surface of gameplay AI programming, but if you reached the end of this book, you are suited for any challenge you may encounter in the future. Good luck, have fun!

Other Books You May Enjoy

If you enjoyed this book, you may be interested in these other books by Packt:

Unity 2018 Artificial Intelligence Cookbook - Second Edition
Jorge Palacios

ISBN: 9781788626170

- Create intelligent pathfinding agents with popular AI techniques such as A* and A*mbush
- Implement different algorithms for adding coordination between agents and tactical algorithms for different purposes
- Simulate senses so agents can make better decisions, taking account of the environment
- Explore different algorithms for creating decision-making agents that go beyond simple behaviors and movement
- Create coordination between agents and orchestrate tactics when dealing with a graph or terrain
- Implement waypoints by making a manual selector

Unity 2018 Cookbook - Third Edition
Matt Smith

ISBN: 9781788471909

- Get creative with Unity's shaders and learn to build your own shaders with the new Shader Graph tool
- Create a text and image character dialog with the free Fungus Unity plugin
- Explore new features integrated into Unity 2018, including TextMesh Pro and ProBuilder
- Master Unity audio, including ducking, reverbing, and matching pitch to animation speeds
- Work with the new Cinemachine and timeline to intelligently control camera movements
- Improve ambiance through the use of lights and effects, including reflection and light probes
- Create stylish user interfaces with the UI system, including power bars and clock displays

Leave a review - let other readers know what you think

Please share your thoughts on this book with others by leaving a review on the site that you bought it from. If you purchased the book from Amazon, please leave us an honest review on this book's Amazon page. This is vital so that other potential readers can see and use your unbiased opinion to make purchasing decisions, we can understand what our customers think about our products, and our authors can see your feedback on the title that they have worked with Packt to create. It will only take a few minutes of your time, but is valuable to other potential customers, our authors, and Packt. Thank you!

Index

Printed in Great Britain
by Amazon